QUESTIONS TO A ZEN MASTER

OTHER BOOKS BY TAISEN DESHIMARU PUBLISHED IN ENGLISH:

THE VOICE OF THE VALLEY, 1979
THE ZEN WAY TO THE MARTIAL ARTS, 1982

Translated and edited by Nancy Amphoux

E.P. DUTTON | NEW YORK

The calligraphy in this book is by Taisen Deshimaru Roshi.

Published in the United States by E. P. Dutton,
a division of NAL Penguin Inc.,
2 Park Avenue, New York, N.Y. 10016.

Library of Congress Cataloging in Publication Data

Deshimaru, Taisen.
Questions to a Zen master.

Translation of Questions à un maitre zen.
1. Zen Buddhism—Addresses, essays, lectures. I. Title.
BQ9266.D4813 1985 294.3'927 84-18746

ISBN: 0-525-48141-9

Published simultaneously in Canada
by Fitzhenry & Whiteside Limited, Toronto

3 5 7 9 10 8 6 4

W

CONTENTS

問答

TRANSLATOR'S NOTE

ABOUT TAISEN DESHIMARU AND HIS MISSION

Taisen Deshimaru was a Soto Zen monk who came to France from Japan in 1967 and settled in Paris. He died in Tokyo in April 1982.

His master was Kodo Sawaki, a great reformer in the first part of this century, who cut through the forests of doctrine, ceremony, and immobility of present-day Zen in Japan, where it had become frozen in the role of a sociological institution weighted down by its past. Sawaki went back to Dogen Zenji himself, the thirteenth-century founder of Soto Zen who is now beginning to emerge as one of the major religious thinkers and leaders of all time.

Taisen Deshimaru lived an "ordinary" life. He went to a university, got a job, married, and had children. Religious forces were at work in him from childhood, however, and he followed his master for many years while continuing to grapple with the everyday problems of everybody. He wanted to be ordained, but Kodo Sawaki told him to stay as he was in order to have the experience of people who were not isolated by the monastic life; in that way he would be able to offer a teaching that was more relevant to them.

He was ordained in due course, received the Dharma transmission, and after his master's death departed for Europe as a Soto Zen missionary.

Deshimaru arrived in Paris by the Trans–Siberian Railway, alone. In the fifteen years he spent in Europe he taught *zazen*, the practice of Zen, tirelessly, day after day. He traveled and lectured constantly. At the end of fifteen years he had several thousand disciples in Europe, North America (including Canada), South America, and North Africa, and over 100 *dojos* had been founded to practice and extend his teaching. He had a temple in Paris and another, larger one near Blois in the Loire Valley.

Deshimaru's personality was unique: blustery, sensitive, truculent, subtle, and inimitable. Its greatest strength lay in the boundless universal energy he transmitted, and in itself there is nothing inimitable about that—as he explains in this book. His closest disciples are continuing his mission exactly as he taught them.

ABOUT ZEN

Zen Buddhism is Mahayana Buddhism, the Greater Vehicle. It is the Buddhism of the *bodhisattva,* the person who remains in "the world" by choice, to help other people rather than to devote himself or herself to a personal salvation. Zen cannot be confined within any concept or expressed by thought. It must be practiced; it is, essentially, an experience.

The philosophical side of Zen Buddhism bears no relation to a closed, highly structured system of thought. It is the transmission of concepts forged by an experience over two thousand years old, which is at the same time fresh every day—the experience of awakening.

It uses a few formulas, a handful of key words, to give sense and direction to the whole field of experience. The words ring together and resound; they point to, without diluting, the uncatchable stream of reality. They illuminate everyday existence, apprehended at its roots.

In Soto Zen the master does not teach by lectures or sermons alone; he regularly holds exchanges of questions and answers with the students. The atmosphere on these occasions, these *mondo* (*mon* = question; *do* = answer), is playful and profound, intent and open-ended, all at once.

ABOUT THIS BOOK

This book contains a selection of questions and answers from twelve years of mondo. It is a rather unusual text. There are many repetitions, the same words are used in different ways, the sentences are for the most part short and extremely simple, and the vocabulary often elementary. People in search of "consistency" will find Deshimaru Roshi's answers irritatingly confusing and fluid; impatient people may think he is saying the same thing over and over; people who are fussy about precision in language will gnash their teeth at what seem to be unnatural usages of "subjective" and "objective," for instance, or at what looks like obstinate ignorance in the use of "spirit" when "attitude" is obviously what is meant.

There are several things that can be said.

First, the words of these replies are not quite words in the ordinary sense. They are unrehearsed, unrevised public speech in the ever-shifting context of times and places. Second, Deshimaru Roshi spoke "Zen-glish"—that is to say, a unique mixture of his rudimentary schoolboy English overlaid with what his Japanese dictionaries told him were possible translations for more sophisticated terms, what his French disciples thought was probably closest to what he wanted to say, and what his interpreters (and their transcribers) could manage to produce in the way of grammatically intelligible sentences in French (or German or Italian or Spanish, as the case may be). The English-speaking translator of the book, who listened to him for nine years, can often remember his actual words, and that adds yet another factor to the equation. It is not surprising if the result is a little disconcerting.

Deshimaru Roshi insisted that his words be taken down exactly as he spoke them, however, and he knew what he was doing. If the word "spirit" turns up where one might think "attitude" was more sensible, it is because he was trying to teach his disciples a new attitude toward spirit.

Deshimaru Roshi had an extraordinarily supple voice—big, rough, soft, cavernous, to suit the occasion. I have put occasional phrases into italics, corresponding to his own emphasis.

The repetitions have been left in, not out of any concern for realism but because they are part of his thought and approach. That thought was always precise, not vague, but as it was not a kind of thought with which we have much experience, his approach seems roundabout. Reading attentively, however, one can begin to sense what that thought was, once the mind has had to discard all the rational-logical representations of what it was not.

Through this book the reader can become acquainted with

a teaching—a philosophy, a religion, an ethic, a life-style, an experience: none of these terms is adequate so best call it a teaching—as it was imparted by the first Zen patriarch of the West. That teaching is as old as the hills yet has never been more relevant than it is amid the planetary turmoil we are experiencing here and now.

INTRODUCTION

ZAZEN, THE WAKEFUL POSTURE OF AWAKENING

The secret of Zen* is the practice of *zazen.* Zazen is difficult, I know. But, practiced daily, it is a very effective way of expanding consciousness and developing intuition. Zazen releases and mobilizes energy; it is also the posture of awakening. While practicing one must not try to achieve or obtain anything; there is no object, only concentration on posture, breathing, and attitude of mind.

Posture. Seated in the middle of the *zafu** (a round cushion), one crosses the legs in full or half-lotus position. If this is impossible, the legs are simply crossed without placing either foot on the opposite thigh, but it is essential that both knees press firmly against the floor. In the lotus position, the feet pressing against the thighs activate major acupuncture points corresponding to meridians of the liver, gall bladder, and kidneys. The samurai of old automatically stimulated these centers by the pressure of their thighs against the flanks of their horse.

At the level of the fifth lumbar vertebra, the pelvis is tipped slightly forward; the waist is hollowed slightly but the back is straight. The knees push down toward the earth, and the head pushes up toward the sky. The chin must be drawn in, which means that the nape of the neck is pressed up and back. The abdomen is relaxed, the nose directly over the navel. The body is like a drawn bow, the mind its arrow.

After assuming this position, the fists (closed around the thumb) are placed on the thighs near the knees, fingers facing up, and the body sways, leaning neither forward nor back, seven or

*Words followed by an asterisk are explained in the glossary beginning on page 139.

eight times to the right and left, each time reducing the movement until it comes to rest at the point of vertical balance. Then . . . *gassho* *—that is, the hands are placed together, palms facing, at shoulder level, the arms remaining horizontal. Gassho is the gesture of respect and reconciliation, the creation of balance, union.

Then, the left hand is placed palm upwards in the right, little fingers touching the abdomen. The tips of the thumbs touch, and slight pressure is exerted to maintain a horizontal line along the top of the thumbs—neither mountain nor valley.

The shoulders are thrown slightly back and down, but fall naturally. The tip of the tongue touches the palate behind the upper teeth. The eyes look down, about one yard ahead; in fact, they are looking inside. Half-closed, they focus on nothing, even if, intuitively, they see everything.

Breathing is most important. Everything that lives, breathes. In the beginning is the breath. Zen breathing is like no other kind. Its chief aim is to establish a slow, powerful, natural rhythm. If you concentrate on breathing out, long, deep, and gently, and fix your attention on the posture, then the breathing in will take care of itself. The air is expelled slowly and silently, while the pressure of the movement exerts a powerful downward force in the abdomen. You "push down on the intestines," thereby massaging the internal organs. The masters compare Zen breathing to the moo of a cow or the first breath of a newborn baby.

Attitude of mind. Correct breathing can follow only from correct posture. In the same way, the right attitude of mind flows naturally from a profound concentration on posture and breathing. Whatever has "wind" lives long, intensely, and tranquilly. The practice of proper breathing enables nervous reactions to be neutralized, instincts and emotions controlled, and mental activity directed.

Circulation within the brain is significantly improved. The cortex rests and the conscious stream of thoughts ceases, while blood is freed to irrigate deeper levels. They wake from their half-slumber and their activity confers a sense of well-being, serenity, and calm, very close to deep sleep yet fully awake. The nervous system is relaxed, the "primitive" brain active. One is receptive, attentive to the highest degree, through every cell in the body. One thinks with the body, unconsciously; all duality and contradictions are left behind, and there is no needless expense of energy. So-called primitive peoples still have an active "old" brain. In developing our kind of civilization we have educated the intellect, refined and complicated it, and lost the strength, intuition, and wisdom that derive from the inner nucleus of the brain. That is why Zen is a priceless treasure for people today, or at least for those who have eyes to see and ears to hear. Through the regular practice of zazen they are given the opportunity to become new by returning to the origins of life. By grasping the very root of existence, they can accede to a normal condition of body and mind (which are one).

When seated in zazen, the images, thoughts, mental constructions arising from the unconscious are allowed to float past like clouds in the sky, with no resistance and no hanging back. Like shadows before a mirror, the emanations of the subconscious drift back and forth, and vanish away. And one reaches the deep unconscious *hishiryo**—where there is no thought, beyond all thought, true purity.

Zen is very simple and at the same time hard to understand. It is a matter of effort and repetition—like life. Sitting there with nothing to do, with no object or desire for profit, if your posture, breathing, and attitude of mind are in harmony, you can understand true Zen, you can perceive the nature of Buddha.

shu do, the middle way

THE MIDDLE WAY

Your expression, "Zen is beyond religion," could be taken to mean that Zen is supposed to take the place of all religions, to supplant them. What do you really mean?

Religions remain what they are. Zen is meditation. Meditation is the foundation of every religion. People today feel an intense need to go back to the source of religious life, to the pure essence in the depths of themselves which they can discover only through actually experiencing it. They also need to be able to concentrate their minds in order to find the highest wisdom and freedom, which is spiritual in nature, in their efforts to deal with the influences of every description imposed upon them by their environment.

Human wisdom alone is not enough, it is not complete. Only universal truth can provide the highest wisdom. *Take away the word Zen and put Truth or Order of the Universe in its place.*

At what point in the history of Buddhism did Zen begin?

When Buddha woke up under the Bodhi tree*.

Afterward it was influenced very strongly by traditional Indian philosophies and religions, and it hardened into scholasticism and asceticism, as in the case of the Theravada* system.

After that, Bodhidharma* left India to transplant the true Zen into new soil, in China. And then Buddhism grew old in China, just as it is declining today in Japan. The essence of Buddhism is the posture of zazen. But in China and Japan zazen is no longer being practiced and that is why I have brought it again to fresh ground here in Europe.

It is often said that Buddhism is the Middle Way, the way of balance, but in the West the middle way means middle-class morality. Can you say something about the "middle way" in Zen?

The middle way does not mean finding yourself between two pretty women and kissing both of them. That's not it. Nor is the middle way cowardice, fear, and inertia; it is not tepid and indecisive. Do not misunderstand it: it embraces opposites, it integrates and goes beyond all contradictions, it is beyond every dualism, even beyond every synthesis. The final verse of the *Hannya Shingyo** sutra* is "Go, go, beyond, together, beyond the beyond to the shore of *satori,** to the wisdom of the Buddha"—that is, the concrete intuition of the fundamental unity of all things: subject and object, body (or matter) and spirit, form and void . . .

In Buddhism the middle way means not setting up an opposition between subject and object. The chief characteristic of European civilization is dualism. Materialism, for example, is opposed to spiritualism. Westerners are very fond of doctrines, of isms. Buddhism, they say, and Christianity. Their isms express the relative positions of what are taken to be distinct entities, but in reality the material and spiritual are one and cannot stand in opposition to each other. Both materialism and communism have opposed Christianity; but communism is not complete either, because it looks only at the material aspect of things, while Christianity looks only at the spiritual aspect and is just as incomplete. Some Christians are different, but for most traditional Christians their religion has to do with the spirit only.

Spirit or mind and body are one thing, like the two sides of a sheet of paper. In everyday life they cannot be separated. One person is drawn to the mental or spiritual, another to the material or physical.

If you want to understand, you must find the middle way. Spiritual is material and material becomes spiritual. Mind exists in every one of our cells and ultimately mind itself is body and the body itself is mind. The only things left in the end are activity and energy; they are not dualistic.

The middle way integrates everything. The highest dimension of all is *mushotoku,** the middle way. Zen is the middle way.

But you must not misunderstand the word "middle": it

means, in regard to material and spiritual, that you must embrace both, like the front and back of a sheet of paper. That's what makes Zen hard to understand.

The middle way is the way beyond. Thesis, antithesis, synthesis: that is the form in which reasoning in the West is always set out. If material = thesis and spiritual = antithesis, then Zen lives the middle way, that of synthesis. Beyond synthesis.

Faith is important in Buddhism, and in Zen there are various objects of faith—zazen, or the kesa,* *or the master. But what is faith?*

Whatever you like. Each person is different. The object of faith differs for each individual. Each person must know and recognize for himself or herself what is his or her object of faith. You must believe in whatever impresses you most deeply. I cannot say, I cannot decide objectively. This is very important. In almost all religions you are told that you have to believe this or that, or in God or Buddha. I do not agree. You have to find for yourself, in yourself. The teacher can lead you to the river's edge but cannot drink in your place, or compel you to drink either. That is a subjective problem.

So I answer, whatever you like. The most important thing is to believe. Believe in what is highest, ultimate. What is true? It is for the wisdom of the spirit to decide.

God, Buddha, the Cross . . . People usually believe according to their genes, their heredity, education, family environment, physical habits. But in the end . . .

The dog follows its master, it forgets everything else when it sees its master. Its brain changes; it is faithful, it believes in its master. True, deep love is important in faith.

In the end, I cannot decide your faith for you. You must decide yourself. It is not just a question of form. I happen to be a Zen monk and, like Dogen* and Nagarjuna,* I believe in the kesa, the garment transmitted by Buddha. That is an eternal transmission. If you want to have faith in Buddha you can, but I cannot decide for you. You must find the answer by yourself.

Does one have to give up one's own religion to follow Zen?

As you like. *You must choose for yourself.* You must look for the essence here and now, decide what is important for yourself. What is the solution to your problems?

Too often religions are no more than decoration. You're supposed to learn all the texts, the order of all the ceremonies; but all that is unimportant. Religions and philosophies have relied too much on the imagination, and that is why they are growing weak. You must cut away the decoration and look for what is important. Find the true essence of all religions.

Does the concept of sin exist for someone who practices Zen?

The problem of sin is not the same in Christianity as it is in Buddhism.

In Christianity there is Original Sin. Adam, Eve, the apple and the serpent. In Buddhism every existence possesses the nature of God or Buddha; this is a very different concept and one that is extremely difficult to explain. All existence, even a stone, everything material, animal, vegetable, everything in its origins possesses the nature of Buddha.

In Oriental philosophy there are two schools of thought. One believes that wickedness is in man's original nature. But the one larger in number believes that what exists at the origin of consciousness, for everything and everyone, is good. That is particularly true of Buddhism. Everybody has Buddha nature, but it is altered by environment and *karma*. * One might say that karma is something like sin; it is transmitted to us by our parents and ancestors and changes our originally pure mind. That is what makes evil exist. When there is no more karma you can return to your normal, original state.

If you practice zazen, your karma comes to an end and sin disappears. It would be very complicated to explain more. The infant in its mother's womb, for example, is sinless, but it already bears the karma of all its ancestors in its blood.

The night before last there was a boy here who was practicing zazen for the first time; he said, "I have just understood what real silence is. Until tonight I have never spent one whole hour in silence in my life. The only time I'm quiet is when I'm in bed and sometimes I even talk in my sleep! But zazen, that is real silence." I said to him, "You were quiet in your mother's womb; that was silence, too." But he said, "My mother talks all the time,

I have a bad karma. I always want to be talking and it's hard for me to keep quiet even in zazen."

But everybody's true origin is silence; you must understand that. *Only silence is your true origin.*

Silence first, then incessant talking. For twenty, thirty, fifty or sixty years you have been talking nonstop. So then you get completely exhausted and return to complete silence again in your coffin. So silence is what goes on eternally. What you have that is eternal is your consciousness of silence, the normal condition of your mind. That is *ku,* * *nirvana.* * The true origin. In Zen we say that we must go back to the original silence, as in Christianity they say we must go back to the state before sin.

If you practice zazen you return to the state before sin.

Why are you always talking about going back to the origin instead of waking up to what lies ahead?

What is waking up? Up to what? Westerners always have these notions of illumination. Yes: Satori means "awakening." People like the idea of waking up; but to what? It's easier to go back. The newborn baby is pure. It has true freedom, it's not at all complicated, doesn't need to make love, gets its food from its mother, cries when it feels like it . . . It doesn't think.

We have to understand what freedom is. If you think with your forebrain all the time, you become complicated; that is how European philosophy got so complicated.

We must go back to the origin of the human being. It's difficult. A *koan* * . . .

Can you say that tigers or cats, animals in general, live true Zen?

Yes, animals live true Zen. And because animals are that way, humans must represent a further development from them. Pigeons are extremely simple, very peaceable, not at all complicated. Sometimes you should follow the animals' way of life, but you must also make use of your human forebrain.

Westerners like to be on one side or the other; either they are all for religion or they detest it—always the same old story of oppositions. What we must do is harmonize religion with communism, American assets with the Arab spirit. If you are always in conflict and battle you can never find true peace. So there needs to be a theory in between. Nobody has found it yet. Only Zen can do it.

That is the principle of the five propositions of Buddhism: there are thesis, antithesis, and synthesis, but not only them. There are also the harmonization of the whole and the embracing and transcending of all contradictions.

sho ji, birth–death; samsara
(the cycle of reincarnation)

HUMAN BEINGS

EGO

What is the ego?

The ego is the ego. It's zazen . . . as in "Know thyself."

I am always saying, You must understand the ego . . . and in the end, there is no ego, *the ego has no substance.* Where are you going to locate this substance? In the nose? The brain? The navel? The head? Hard to say. In the mind? But what is the mind? It has become a problem, the biggest problem of psychology, philosophy, and religion.

I have explained that we have no noumenon, no permanent substance. The ego changes with every second that goes by; yesterday's ego, today's ego . . . they're not the same. Our body changes, our cells change too. When you take a bath, for example, all the dead cells of your skin are washed away. Our brain, our mind changes; that of the adult is not the same as it was in the child.

So where does the ego exist? It is one with the cosmos. It is not only the body, the mind, but it is God, Buddha, the fundamental cosmic force.

To find eternity is not egotism; it is truth, true noumenon. That is the true religion we must create.

Our life is connected to the cosmic power and stands in a relation of interdependence with all other existences. *We cannot live by ourselves,* we are dependent upon nature, air, water. So we must not become selfish . . . That is the great satori.

It is useless to be egotistical because every ego is in a relationship of interdependence with the world and with all things. So there is no need to keep things for oneself.

That is very important.

In his *Essays,* Montaigne wrote that everybody else was always looking outward, but he wanted to look within. It is necessary to turn your eyes inward, even though most people only look outside. Today more than ever before we must look into ourselves. To look at an object is easy, to look at the subject is not so easy.

You have said that we had to have an ego and also be beyond the ego. What does that mean?

It looks like a contradiction. But having a strong ego is not the same thing as having an egotistical ego.

You must have confidence in yourself. You must find your real ego and at the same time let go of your ego. If you continue zazen your true ego will become strong and you will find your own self. You are not interchangeable with another body. You are not composed solely of organs and hair. *You have your own originality. But to find it you must abandon your ego,* abandon everything so that only the true ego remains.

Each person has a karma, transports mud and dust. But when all that is cleared away you can find your true originality.

Being different from others means being alone too. Is it possible, through zazen, to learn how to be alone, to accept loneliness?

If you continue zazen, your characteristics change. Your sad face is completely transformed, unconsciously, naturally and automatically. It's the Way that changes you, brings you back to a normal condition.

You should not try to escape from loneliness by becoming too "diplomatic" or depending on other people. Solitude is good. Zen is solitude. Becoming intimate with yourself during zazen means being completely alone and also with the others, with the cosmos.

What is individuality?

Individuality and a strong ego are different. Coming back to one's own originality is very important; you and I are not the same. You are only you. You must find your own you. Through zazen you can end your bad karma.

Nowadays education standardizes everybody; it has become mass education. Even parents are unable to see the underlying individualities of their own children.

Through zazen you can realize that individuality and make it strong. The duty of a religious person is to teach that to other people. Nowadays only the intellect is educated, not the whole individual.

You say that when we practice zazen we are Buddha or God, and you also say that we must abandon the ego. How can the two be reconciled?

If you abandon your ego, you become God or Buddha! When you let go of everything, when you have shed everything, *when you have finished with your own personal consciousness, then you are God or Buddha* . . . When everything else is finished. There's nothing contradictory in that.

But if you tell yourself, "Now I have abandoned everything and I am God," if you think you are God, then you aren't God at all. That's what counts, and everybody gets it wrong. We cannot certify that we are God. If I say, "I have satori," then I'm just crazy.

A crazy person always says, "I'm not crazy at all, I'm in my own normal condition." If the crazy person said, "Maybe I'm not quite right. Maybe I'm making a mistake," then that person would not be so crazy after all and could surely be cured. But if he says he is God or Buddha then his madness is incurable.

When everything is done with, thrown away, one becomes God or Buddha.

For someone looking at a zazen posture, the posture itself is Buddha or God. The authentic thing is unconscious.

That is a good question and everybody gets it wrong.

That's why I am forever saying that when you practice zazen you don't need to say to yourself, "I must become like this or like that." *Unconsciously, naturally, automatically, you can become it.* That is the essence of Soto* Zen.

Mushotoku . . . without any goal, without any object, just concentrating on the posture of zazen.

You wrote that when we practice zazen we are in our coffin. But even though we know we don't exist we still have the feeling of existing!

Of course. We're not dead! If you did not feel your own existence you would be completely dead. What I said was that you should practice zazen as though you were entering your coffin. It's an illustration.

Why is death always a central problem for religions? Because people are egotistical and the ego is important. *If you can solve the question of death, then you completely abandon the ego.* If a person is not afraid of death, that person is not an egotist. So I say you must practice zazen "in your coffin." True *zazen* is letting go of the ego. The ego doesn't exist. No noumenon. It's satori.

What is an ego? Ears, nose, heart, brain? Is it separate from the rest? Everybody is egotistical, but when all is said and done we are "lived" by the cosmic order. You cannot stop your heart from beating; it's impossible. You don't want to think but thoughts rise up. We live through interdependence, through the power of interdependence. *Substance does not exist. So it is possible to let go of it.*

If you understand that, if you let go of the ego, then you can become completely happy. But so long as one remains attached to oneself one cannot be happy.

Egotists catch diseases, they are not free. But if they become less egotistical they can become happy. All true religions teach that.

In Christianity Jesus sacrificed himself for everybody else and so he is still living. Religions teach that we should abandon the ego in order to help, to serve others; and that is exactly the hardest thing for a human being to do. Our modern civilization could hardly be more egotistical. And people are unhappy. Abandoning the ego is difficult, but it is necessary, in order to influence others.

During zazen when you're afraid to abandon your ego, what is the right attitude to adopt?

It's not necessary to think about it. Go on practicing; that is what matters. The shape of your face appears reflected in the mirror;

you reflect yourself, you can see and understand your mind, you can know your true ego.

I don't understand the mirror symbol in the Hokyo Zanmai*: *"The reflection, the image, is me, but I am not the reflection."*

During zazen the ego-subject can look at the ego-object, and vice versa. We can realize that we are not so wonderful, sometimes we're even worse than other people, because in deep zazen our true desires are revealed and we can see them fully.

We always have two egos, but that doesn't mean that we have a dual personality.

The objective ego is the good spirit. It is the spirit of God, it's the spirit of Buddha, the one that sees. We can observe ourselves in depth, and wake up and reflect. At that moment we become pure, and we can become more pure.

In everyday living we can't be really pure. But after a long time, with the experience gained through the practice of zazen, our life becomes purified even if it is made very impure by the fact that we have too many desires. In everyday living we cannot be completely pure because of our karma. Each person has his or her own karma. For perfect purity, the coffin is best! That is why religion is necessary for people who are alive.

If we have known the religious life, the connected life, then the objective ego will organize a good subjective ego and the mind will become fresh and free.

Master Dogen said, "I am not other people."

That is a great story and a famous koan.

I am not others. It is I who must act. If I do not practice I cannot explain.

The quote comes from the famous story about the mushrooms:

Master Dogen had gone to China to find true wisdom, to understand Zen. He studied many things but he did not really understand. In those days the religion of Buddhism, of Zen, was very widespread in China and he went from one temple to another. Nevertheless, he was not satisfied with the teaching he received so he decided to go home to Japan. Then one day he came to another temple. It was summer, and very hot. There was a very old monk there working, drying mushrooms. Old and frail as he was, he was spreading the mushrooms out in the sun.

Master Dogen saw him and asked him, "Why are you working? You are an old monk and a superior of the temple. You should get younger people to do this work. It is not necessary for you to work. Besides, it is extremely hot today. Do that another day." Master Dogen was young then.

The old monk's answer was most interesting and has become famous in the history of Soto Zen.

It was a satori for Master Dogen.

The monk said to him, "You have come from Japan, young man, you are intelligent and you understand Buddhism, but you do not understand the essence of Zen. If I do not do this, if I do not work here and now, who could understand? I am not you, I am not others. Others are not me. So others cannot have the experience. If I don't work, if I do not have this experience here and now, I cannot understand. If a young monk helped me to do the work, if I were to stand by and watch him, then I could not have the experience of drying these mushrooms. If I said, 'Do this, do that. Put them here or there,' I could not have the experience. I could not understand the act that is here and now.

"I am not others and others are not me." Master Dogen was startled, and he suddenly understood. True, he was highly intelligent. He said to himself, "I had better spend a little more time here in China." He had studied in books, he had looked with his brain and he spent all his time thinking, but just then he understood: "If I do not have the experience I cannot understand true Zen. Zen cannot be apprehended by the brain."

The old monk and Dogen communicated to each other. Master Dogen was startled and deeply affected. However, he went on: "Why are you drying those mushrooms today? Do it some other day." To which the old monk answered, "Here and now is very important. These mushrooms can't be dried another day. If this moment is lost it will not be possible to dry them: perhaps it will rain, perhaps there won't be enough sun. You need a hot day to dry mushrooms, so today is the right time to do it. Now go away, I have to work! If you want to find true Zen, go see my master in the *dojo.*"* So Master Dogen went to see the old monk's master and learn from him. At last he understood true Zen, which he had never been able to understand before.

Master Dogen spent a year in this temple, then received the kesa of transmission. Afterward, he went back to Japan. But the founding principle of his philosophy always remained, "Here and now, other people are not me, I am not other people. If I do not practice I cannot understand. If somebody else does something, I cannot be in what he does." That's the first point.

The second is "*shikantaza**—only zazen." Koans are not necessary, thinking is not necessary: only zazen. Descartes said, "I think, therefore I am." I say, "I do not think, that is why I exist."

If you create your own categories, if you think too much, you limit your consciousness. But consciousness is as deep as the cosmos. It is connected to the cosmos. If you don't think, your consciousness becomes eternal, cosmic. That is extremely important. If you think during zazen you cannot reach the cosmic consciousness because you limit yourself. You cannot reach the limitless.

When you don't think rationally, you can think unconsciously. If I do not think, I exist here; I do not think, therefore I am.

> *But we exist whether we think or not. Both are important. Which comes first?*

If we are not thinking we exist eternally because then consciousness is boundless, eternal. It goes on all the way to God, Buddha, the cosmos, truth.

Once the ego has disappeared there is no more duality. As soon as there is myself and others, that is duality. *When there is no more me there are no more others; there is interdependence.* That is nonthought.

You should not restrict your thinking with words and phrases. When you create your own categories the words do not fit. Westerners are always using their vocabulary to create categories, and sometimes what they come up with are contradictions. *In language, there are always two.*

If I say, "What's that?" the only word is, "That is that." If I say "What's that?" and you say, "It's a *kyosaku*,"* it would be just as true to say, "It's a piece of wood." "It's oak" would also be right.

Zen discussions are always like that. One monk says, "The flame is moving." The next says, "No, it's not the flame, it's the air that's moving." The third, who is cleverer than the other two, says, "No, it's neither the flame nor the wind, it's your mind that's moving." And in the end the fourth person says, "It is neither the wind nor the flame nor your mind."

You must understand why others are not you. *If I cannot do it, I cannot explain it.* I am not other people. I am what I am. I am myself. It's not necessary to follow the others.

There are many meanings. "I am me." "It's not necessary to follow the others." I have to decide by myself. I must do what I do myself. Others are not me, it's true, but it is also true that my mind and your mind have the same substance. I am like the sky and the earth. When you let go of everything, you become others. That is abandoning the ego. Don't get it wrong.

That is the koan of Master Dogen's mushrooms.

KARMA

What is karma?

Karma means "action."

If you strike someone, shoot, point your finger, your gesture has an effect. Just as zazen has an effect, here and now and in the future.

There is the karma of the body, of the mouth and of the consciousness. If you kill a person, even if you are never caught and brought to trial, one day the karma of that act will certainly appear, in your own life or in that of your descendants. This is not a matter of morality.

Zazen is the best karma: the body's posture is simple and exact. You are silent and your mind is beyond thought. Karma disappears. It's not necessary to try to get away from it or cover it up. But good karma, on the other hand—that you must try to create.

During zazen you let your dreams and illusions go by, and they disappear. Not-thinking doesn't mean sleep; it means thought that is fresh. Zazen refreshes the brain, the features of the face become noble. When you rest the forebrain, where rational thought takes place, infinite wisdom arises . . .

Do karma and fate mean the same thing?

No, they are not the same.

Karma equals action. Action of our body, our consciousness, our speech. If I strike you with my fist, for example, that is karma, an action that becomes karma. When we speak we create karma. When we think we create a karma that plants a seed in the *alaya** consciousness. If you steal that becomes karma, a karma that will not be good and that will bear evil fruit.

At a *sesshin** once, one of my disciples did not behave well —too much sex, too much drinking—and the day he left he had an accident in his car with a young lady. That time, karma returned to the surface very quickly. Even little things reappear. Whatever we do with our body, speech or thought, very certainly karma is created.

When you are born you have a karma: that of your forebears, your grandparents, for example. But karma can be changed, whereas fate is a constant.

If you practice zazen your karma changes completely, it becomes better.

During zazen your body creates the highest karma, because the posture is the highest act. It's the same way with speech: words are not really so good, and being silent is the best karma. The consciousness during zazen is also the highest and creates the highest karma. In this way you can transform your bad destiny into good destiny.

Karma is one of the basic principles of Buddhism, although the problem of how to change one's karma exists in other religions, too. How does one disconnect oneself from one's bad karma and have a better karma? I think zazen is the best method.

Consciousness is very important. Other religions and philosophies concern themselves only with the karma of body and speech. But how do you create good karma of thought? By means of hishiryo consciousness.

Where does one's personal karma begin?

Here and now. It is manifesting itself all the time, at every instant, even during zazen. It ceases to appear only in the grave.

And when you're asleep?

You dream; that is karma coming back to the surface. You move, you scratch yourself; even in bed people perform actions. When they have had too much to drink they snore. Karma arises, manifests itself everywhere. That is what karma is.

If you have come here and practiced zazen, then your past karma has surely come to the surface. The very fact of coming here means that a good karma in the past incited you to come.

It is not so easy to choose deliberately to perform nothing but good deeds. But practicing zazen is absolute action. That alone creates an infinite good karma, and that karma too will inevitably come back to the surface. Even if a person practices zazen only once and never comes again, that karma will influence his existence later on.

If someone has a bad karma, how can he or she be interested in zazen?

Everybody has a bad karma. You too have a bad karma. Karma is not a monolith. There are many different kinds of karma. The source is completely pure, the tributaries are muddy. Every one of your thoughts, every one of your actions influences your body, your face. *Every single thing becomes karma.* If you tell a lie you create karma.

Chanting the *Hannya Shingyo* creates good karma. Shutting one's mouth in one's everyday life creates good karma. People are forever talking. Silence is a good karma.

If you have a longing for fine food and don't eat it you create good karma. If you drink too much whisky or cognac and then stop, that becomes good karma. But every single thing creates karma.

Practicing zazen is the greatest, the absolute karma. But karma is not just one thing. The two sides of the scales must always balance, one good thing weighing against one bad one.

What does it mean to "confess one's bad karma"?

It means to observe your past actions: "There I was good, there I was bad." Through the practice of zazen one can become more and more profoundly aware of one's weak points, bad sides—and I don't mean in terms of morality only. You cannot lie to yourself. That is confession.

"I keep practicing zazen and the more I practice the more I see that I am the worst creature on earth." If you understand that, then you are becoming truly profound. If you understand your ego objectively, you are like God.

That is the highest dimension. During zazen you can understand. It is not necessary to confess to other people, only to oneself. That is the best confession.

A person who is really crazy cannot understand that he is crazy, but a madman who understands that he is mad is not so crazy. The normal condition of the mind is satori!

When you know that you have faults, bad features, is it better to combat them deliberately or forget about them in silence and let them change automatically?

Both. Westerners are forever inventing distinctions and creating dualism, but in reality both attitudes are necessary.

To want to change deliberately is to have a goal and that is futile. At the first obstacle, you stumble. Sometimes, however, it is good to have a goal.

If you want to understand truly and profoundly, you must have nothing. Practice shikantaza. If you are continually struggling to achieve something, you will become like an ascetic, a hermit in the mountains. That is just another form of egotism.

If you continue to practice zazen you will be beyond qualities and defects.

Like the painter, you have to let go of your ego in order to produce a masterpiece.

Concentrate without any goal here and now, and do not make a goal of wanting to change.

What are good deeds?

The practice of zazen is the only absolute [illegible]

Even if you have the desire to perform [illegible] deeds, they are not so easy to perform in real[illegible] some person, for example. Millions of good deeds [illegible] if you have not freed yourself from a desire to ob[illegible] it will be very difficult for you to perform them.

If you practice zazen you can be kind, can lo[illegible] goal, unconsciously, naturally, automatically. It is not n[illegible]ssary to make a choice using your own personal will. *You can do anything, but you must not choose!*

A lot of people nowadays want to perform good actions. The brain understands: "One should act like this or like that . . . " and it sets up limitations. It is will, your personal will, that tries to dictate, and as a result everything becomes complicated.

If you follow the cosmic order you can create true good karma, by returning to the source of zazen. That is faith. That is the action of true religion.

If you think about it with your personal consciousness, if you must do one thing or another in order to follow the dictates of ethics or morality, then life becomes difficult. You limit your existence and cannot find true freedom.

But if you practice zazen your actions become free—unconsciously, naturally, automatically.

ILLUSIONS, ATTACHMENT, SUFFERING

What is suffering, and why is suffering?

It is only your mind that suffers. If you are anxious you suffer, but if you disconnect the roots of your anxiety your suffering disappears.

Buddha also asked himself that question.

The ego suffers for itself; without it there would be no more suffering. That is the suffering that comes of one's consciousness of life, family, desires, the future. That is why Buddhism recommends that people sever their attachments to family, money, society, and so forth. But this applies only on the level of the spirit, not to actual forms of behavior. If you sever your attachment to your family, then you will be able to love your family truly and profoundly, without egotism.

What creates profound, true love—love without object and without desire for profit, universal and eternal—is understanding the nature of the ego.

Then suffering is pointless.

Love and work no longer create suffering; the roots have been cut, "as in the coffin."

Inside yourself there will be nothing left; the ego abandoned means true happiness.

Outwardly, however, you go on acting, loving, working; there is no contradiction. That is the normal condition, making possible harmony with others through true inner freedom and true simplicity. Religion means following that inner freedom and not some morality or other. *True religion means harmonizing with what is outside, with society, with everything around us.* That is the right place for the *bodhisattva,* * the monk.

Doing away with suffering is the problem of all religions; it is their source and the source of all spiritual life.

Death is the greatest suffering. That is why we need a spiritual life.

How can we escape from the complications of life?

Complications mean not enough wisdom. When you become wise you lose your complications.

If you want to become profound you must live through your complications. If you want to understand Zen, live through a sesshin. If you live through those difficulties, you will be able to understand. It is necessary to experience them in order to become strong. People who have never had any complications have a different face and mind. When people begin to have difficulties —if they understand—they can recover the true simplicity of the child, their true mind, and it becomes impossible for them to be involved in complications again.

Do you have to go through sickness, death, and suffering in order to get to ku?

That is the experience of *mujo,** impermanence, the very wellspring of Buddhism, the original experience of Buddha. How to resolve suffering? The question is at the back of almost all religions. But there is no point in telling oneself, "I must understand suffering and in order to understand I must suffer." You will surely have the experience one time or another in your life. If you practice zazen you can know your suffering objectively. Then time passes, and it is no different from a dream.

In the presence of suffering it is necessary, sometimes, to observe oneself objectively, as in zazen. Then the suffering becomes less important. It fades away, just as desires and pain fade in the moment of death.

Is it possible, sitting in zazen, to sever attachment and desires through control of the mind and posture?

Yes; but not after a single sesshin. That is why you must go on practicing.

It is no easy matter to sever attachment. *Attachment represents karma that has not been manifested.* Intellectually, one can understand that one must sever attachment, but in practice it is extremely hard to do.

If you continue zazen, unconsciously, naturally, automatically, your attachments diminish and in the end, even if you want to attach yourself to something you can no longer do it. Satori.

One of my disciples said to me, "I've got a fiancée and I'm very attached to her. How can I sever that attachment?" I told him, "Have two, three, a dozen fiancées. By that means your attachment will change, become divided, and decrease. In the end you'll be worn out and not at all attached anymore!"

When you continue to practice zazen your willpower, your deliberate intentions, cease to operate. Unconsciously, you become peaceful. When you practice zazen you enter your coffin, where nothing is very important anymore and there is no need for any attachment.

When you are attached to things your actions cannot be balanced because you act with your emotions . . . But through zazen subjective attachments disappear, you can become strong, act firmly and surely, and in harmony. Your inner mind becomes completely calm.

Isn't the desire for the eternal life of the soul a form of attachment?

Yes, everybody has that desire. But not everything in attachment is bad. Attachment to zazen, for instance. Or attachment to satori; that's better than attachment to sex. In fact, it is not really attachment, but a hope, an ideal.

But Buddha became Buddha by severing all his illusions!

Oh, he must have had a few left!

It is not possible to sever everything, not even for Buddha. But in zazen he could see his own karma and gain satori. He saw the root of the evil and so he could understand everything.

One cannot sever everything, even in zazen . . . But one can see in oneself how mistakes are made and that is satori.

During zazen, if you think you have satori you are a little bit crazy. If Buddha had thought that he would not have had satori. But he understood his karma; that was the essential part of his experience.

You must understand your own karma. If you understand it really, if you confess to yourself, you experience satori and you can decrease your karma.

Is freedom something real or is it an illusion?

True freedom is inside the mind. Some people appear to be free but in their minds they are not free at all. I feel free in myself, even though I have to obey the precepts. I don't have so many desires, I live simply. Even when my projects fail, even if my whole mission were a failure, I should still have my *kolomo** and my shaven head and my kesa and I could sleep by the side of the road—a true Zen monk.

People who are ambitious and full of desires are always searching for freedom but they can't find it. They are always worried and sad, their desires keep growing and growing, and in the end they fall ill or become neurotic.

Freedom does not mean doing whatever you like. Too much gratification of desires does not lead to freedom because human desires are limitless.

The best thing is to have fewer desires.

Freedom is different at each age of life and for each karma. Young people should not become narrow-minded by trying to limit their desires. The middle way, balance, is important.

As much as possible, you should sublimate your desires; then freedom comes through a spiritual ideal.

You often say that the greatest freedom comes through zazen, but you also say that it is impossible to do away with all one's illusions. Isn't that a contradiction? How can you reconcile illusions and freedom?

It is possible. Illusions really come to an end only in the coffin, but it is important to regulate, control them. Cutting them off by force—with a chastity belt, for example—simply makes people hysterical.

So, how are we to regulate them through the practice of zazen? Control does not mean cut. In our lives today, for example, we may want to make money so we concentrate on money, but without running after it, without attaching ourselves to money, and we receive it without greed; otherwise, it runs away like the cat. To remain peaceful always, and not anxious, is best. And in that way, through zazen, we can regulate desires as they arise.

What does it mean when you say that satori and illusion are the same?

What I always say is that satori becomes illusion and illusion becomes satori. During zazen, illusions arise, go by, evaporate.

Westerners always make a distinction between illusion and satori. They are always creating categories: good on one side, bad on the other. It's not so simple. Good can become bad and vice versa. Unhappiness can bring happiness and happiness can bring unhappiness.

What is easy does not lead to happiness.

Losing one's illusions can lead to a great satori. One of the sutras says that illusions become the water of satori; the relationship is like that between ice and water. Illusion becomes satori. As it melts, a big piece of ice produces a lot of water, and all the illusions melting away produce satori. But it would be a mistake to believe that because one has a lot of illusions one is going to have a lot of satori, or any satori at all!

Happiness comes after difficulties. The greater the difficulties, the greater the happiness. Young people refuse difficulty and so they are not at all happy. Zazen is difficult but it makes happiness. If you practice zazen regularly, if you have the experience of a sesshin, afterwards you will be very happy in your everyday life.

You suffer during zazen, but you become profound. Your personality becomes richer. But it is not necessary to believe that one must suffer in order to become profound. Zazen is like a mirror; the mirror doesn't change, it is always pure, illusions do not tarnish it!

During zazen one can become aware that one is thinking; one's illusions file past in front of the mirror. *But even if we die we can exist eternally because we have no noumenon, no permanent substance.* That is a koan.

If you can understand that, you will become free and at peace.

When attachments and illusions disappear, what is left?

You don't need to worry about that. You will always have some illusions left. Even when you're asleep you dream; it is hard to disconnect illusions, even during zazen. Total nirvana will exist only in your coffin.

In Mahayana* Buddhism one does not try to sever illusions but rather to transform them, change them into wisdom, purity. That is zazen.

If you continue to practice you will be able to understand. We actually can metamorphose our passions into wisdom. We can reduce the part of error in ourselves. To sever everything is very hard indeed, but to metamorphose it through zazen is possible.

HELPING OTHERS

What is compassion?

There are many degrees and forms of love. Universal love is the deepest. If we really feel sorry for someone we are not just conscious of the person's physical or emotional suffering, their distress. We must become like them, have the same state of mind as they. *Then how should we act, to help, comfort, heal?* We must, always, see things not from our own subjective point of view but by becoming the other, without duality. We must not just love but become identical with the other mind. In love we are always two. Compassion, or *jihi,** is unity.

When I meet you I become you. "How are you? Not so bad?"

Somebody gave me a present yesterday. I must give him twice as much in return. Often, with love, it is impossible to do that, so in the end you escape. True compassion is genuine sympathy. We must forget ourselves and become the other. But compassion must always go hand in hand with wisdom. And wisdom with compassion. A great deal has been written on this subject in China and Japan. The whole world proclaims it, in fact, but in Buddhism it has become a powerful force.

In love there is always duality, opposition between partners. But in compassion the two beings are only one. Love is relative. Compassion is total communion between two beings. But without wisdom love is blind. Nowadays many parents love their children with egotistical attachment, and so the children want to escape. Too much attachment is not true love, true compassion.

You say that Zen wants to reach the highest wisdom and the deepest love, but some people think zazen produces indifference to others, they say it is the opposite of the active charity taught by Christianity. How would you say that zazen develops an attitude of love?

The ultimate dimension, in the very depths of being, the supreme dimension of life, is universal consciousness and love. Each cannot exist without the other. *Truth and love are one and the same thing.* So you can say that the active charity taught by Christianity is included in that dimension and is a direct emanation of it.

Zen Buddhism is also a religion of love because it is the religion of the bodhisattvas who abandon everything to help others, to work for the salvation of others before their own salvation (and in that practice, it goes even further than Christianity). And the first of the precepts is *fuse**—charity—which means more than a material gift; it means giving morally as well, a sacrifice. Not just giving to somebody but giving oneself and giving to God, to Buddha.

But where is the source of this active charity to be found, if not in the knowledge of one's own heart, of one's profound ego, which is that of every other existence, acquired through meditation?

Zen also teaches harmony, harmonizing with others—chanting the sutras together, meditating together, cultivating harmony together.

In Japanese, to be a monk means to harmonize.

Inner spiritual solitude is good but one must always harmonize with, turn toward, others too.

"All go together, beyond the beyond, to the other shore."

Isn't a personal quest for inner freedom selfish in comparison with the quest for freedom for all?

Both are necessary. If I can't solve my own problems I will not be able to help other people solve theirs. I have to free myself of my own problems before I can help other people to free themselves. So both are necessary.

Westerners always want to help other people. Roman Catholics, too, want to help people for their salvation and for their own good. Mahayana Buddhism is the same, except that first we must understand ourselves.

You often say that practicing zazen solves the problem of life and death. But how can it solve the suffering of other people?

First you must solve your own suffering, because if your own brain is not in a normal condition you cannot help other people. You would make them even more complicated than they already are. One day you yourself told me that *samu** (physical labor) helped you to solve your sufferings. "Before I used to suffer a great deal. The poison in my body and mind is now gone." If you practice zazen you can help other people. There's no need to think about it consciously. Practice zazen. Don't complicate things. Then you will be able to solve the sufferings of others. It takes wisdom to be able to help.

How can one help others concretely?

What does "help" mean?

Having no object, no goal is better. If you think, during zazen, "I must help So-and-So and practice zazen now for that purpose," your zazen is not good. To practice zazen with a mushotoku-mind, "no-profit," that is what is most important; beyond any goal, the highest zazen. It's not worth telling yourself, "My zazen must be profound so that I can help other people." Shikantaza means just sitting, without any object. Practice zazen automatically, naturally, unconsciously, and its influence will become infinite. Dogen wrote that if one person practices zazen only one hour, that person influences all the people in the whole world. It is not easy to help other people. Giving them money is not enough.

What matters most is always to remain beyond categories, otherwise one becomes narrow, narrower and narrower.

Hishiryo consciousness is infinite.

What does the sentence, "Give to the rich and take from the poor," mean?

Wealthy people are always afraid that someone is going to ask them for something. It's a psychological phenomenon. On the other hand, it will certainly be a pleasant surprise for them if somebody gives them something. Are you rich or poor?

Poor.

If, being poor, you give something, then that is true charity. Rich people can always make presents, but for you it is a true fuse, a gift of great value, of great price.

At Nara in Japan there is a very great temple called Todai-ji. In that temple there is an enormous statue of Buddha. Master Genjo, its founder, was asked by the emperor to build a big temple; so the priest went to a bridge under which lived many,

many beggars. After bowing down to them he asked them for alms. They were completely bewildered and taken aback. And then they felt very proud.

Every day Genjo came to perform *sampai,** prostrate himself before them; and every day they gave him a little money. Some gave more. And so he began to build the temple. He told them what the statue was to be like and explained that by contributing to the building they would be remembered by history. The statue is of Buddha sitting on a lotus flower.

So the beggars gave him a lot of money and talked about it all day long. Before, they had always been beseeching and complaining, "I'm sick, help me, please." Afterwards, they became truly wise and their words grew profound. They gave away half of everything they begged to build the temple, and they went on giving until it was finished.

What is the difference between Buddha and bodhisattvas?

That is hard to explain. It would take a whole lecture. The bodhisattva is a living Buddha.

In Mahayana Buddhism there is no fear of hell. In Christianity that is the supreme punishment. In Zen, if you have to go to hell you go. If you went to sit beside the Buddha you would have to be practicing zazen all the time and then you wouldn't have so much freedom. So people think that it's better to go to hell! The Zen monk must leap into hell to save those who are suffering. The bodhisattva must leap into the impurities of the social world. Leap, not fall! Falling into the river and diving into the river are completely different things. If you fall into the river your only thought is to save your life. If you dive into the river you swim and then you can save people who are drowning. Bodhisattvas dive into the world to help.

Statues of the Buddha are different from statues of bodhisattvas: Buddha is not decorated, bodhisattvas are. They don't have to cut off their hair. They wear the same clothes as everybody else. They live in society. They don't change their lives. The only difference is on the inside.

Sometimes it is necessary to rub your hands in impurities. There was a monk once who spent his life in jail to help the other prisoners. As his behavior was perfect he was always released after a short time. So he would quickly commit another offense in order to go back to jail. In the end there were no prisoners left except him.

Then there was a Zen master who did the accounts for a house of geishas. The geishas became nuns (there may have been a few nuns who became geishas, too, but the story doesn't say). He would give talks to all the men who came to the house. The men changed completely, too, and many of them became monks. That is also the bodhisattva's vocation. I could give you many examples.

Dogen criticized Rinzai. * *Masters are always criticizing each other. What do you think about criticism?*

To progress, we need discussion. Personal criticism is bad; in fact, it is forbidden. But discussions of different schools, doctrines, philosophies, are necessary. Sometimes, a genuine criticism is beneficial. I like to hear real criticism; it makes me progress. Dogen's criticism of Rinzai was genuine. And if you want to find true Zen, self-criticism is necessary. Not egotistical criticism, but the means of finding what is best for oneself, true religion.

In general, if people are wrong about something, should we let them alone or try to show them their mistakes?

Every person has to understand for himself or herself. You cannot drink for the cow. You can lead it to the river's edge but the cow has to drink for itself. We have to understand by ourselves.

GOOD AND EVIL

What is the Buddhist concept of good and evil?

In the last analysis it is impossible to differentiate between good and evil. The distinction is relevant only from the viewpoint of morality. A robot could perform good or evil, depending on its program. Humans often act the same way. Some think neither good nor evil . . .

Dogs do not perceive colors. *Fish are happy in the sea but humans aren't.* Each thing has its own world, each individual is different. Each has its own god. Your world and the cat's world are not the same. What is good for some is bad for others. In the end, it is impossible to choose. There is the world of young people, the world of old people. For some people making love is good, for others it's bad. But if our minds have no limits they can resolve all contradictions. If you stand on a level that is high enough and look down, nothing is so very, very good or so very, very bad; you are no longer aware of the contradiction.

During zazen you can see and understand everything objectively. If you look subjectively then everything becomes complicated, and you're sad or full of cares. But if your zazen is deep, you enter your coffin and there is no more good or bad. What is so important, when death is in front of you? Nothing is so very important. During zazen you experience your coffin subjectively, and then everything grows calm.

Since it is so hard to distinguish between good and evil, should we avoid taking any positive action in everyday life?

Everyday life and the religious mind are two different things. In society, good and evil exist. Laws are determined by the lowest morality; they have to do with the karma of the actions of body and speech.

If you have evil thoughts, nobody puts you in prison. From the viewpoint of religion, it's different. In religion, thought is important. In Zen what is essential is to be conscious and able to define "how we think."

In everyday life, even if we have evil thoughts but our actions are good, there is no offense. On the other hand, if we have good thoughts but bad actions we go to prison. Action alone is taken into consideration. But ultimately, it is hard to decide what is good and what is bad. Ultimately, everything looks like a dream. Our life is like a dream.

The mind of Buddha sees all things. There, it is not a question of social morality but of the real essence of religions. And at that level, it is not easy to distinguish between good and evil. Moral law and religion are different.

If we can neither choose nor refuse, how can we live a moral life?

Morality is necessary and you should follow it insofar as possible. But morality is not everything. Sometimes it is necessary, sometimes not. *And religion is beyond morality.*

In morality only the actions of body and speech are involved; but the action of the consciousness goes farther than that. How should we think?

We must find true freedom.

For morality, too much sex is not good. But in the *Lotus Sutra,* * for example, it is written that "sexual orgasm is the true, pure spirit of the bodhisattva." Only a master can read this sutra; for you it would be nothing but pornography and it would be dangerous for me to teach it to you. How do we solve the problem of morality? We must not lean either right or left, and we must not worry about leaning right or left. Balance is what is important, and that is what I teach.

What do demons represent in Buddhism?

I have no idea. In Buddhism, God, Buddha, and the devil sometimes have the same face. There is no duality between God and the devil, no separation. They have the same face. Sometimes Buddha becomes the devil and sometimes it's the other way around.

In Christianity God is only one and He is supposed to be able to command the devil. But in the modern world God and the devil are separate and God can no longer command. That is why life has become so difficult. Human beings cannot sever their demon-karma. Even if they don't want to do harm, they go on doing it because of their karma. For some people it's the other way around: even if they want to do wrong they can't. You can have the experience for yourself. This is a big problem and an important point in Buddhism.

On a very high level it is hard to say what is good and what is bad because the true God includes all things, good and evil. It is not possible to say, "You're bad so I don't love you," or, "You're good so I love you." That is not the true Buddha's attitude. Buddhism includes the entire cosmos and all things in it are necessary. If you see with an eternal eye even bad things become good, and good ones bad. The universe includes all things. *If you step into your coffin and look back at your life, it will not look either good or bad to you.*

What is meant by Heaven and Hell?

Read Dante, or the Christian Bible. It's the same in Buddhism. But I turn the question back to you because I cannot decide.

In Zen we must create heaven here and now, not hell. It is we who make heaven or hell in our mind.

When I was a child my mother used to tell me, "If you're bad you'll go to hell. If you're good you'll go to heaven." Then I was afraid but when I grew up I said to myself, "I'll go to hell; people must have more freedom there. I'll become the devil's friend," or, "If I go to heaven with Buddha I'll be forever having arguments with my mother and I won't have any freedom at all." When I was about fifteen or sixteen, I was always arguing with my mother and I had absolutely no desire to go to heaven.

Later, I asked my master Kodo Sawaki* that question. In those days I was a student, and because I had studied science and logic I no longer believed in either place. Kodo Sawaki taught me that heaven and hell are in our mind.

We cannot decide whether they exist or not. Nobody has come back. Once people are in their coffins they don't come back to tell us. But here and now, it is our mind that makes hell and heaven. Master Dogen wrote very deeply on the subject.

We must create heaven here and now. If we suffer, if we doubt, everything can become hell. We must build heaven. If our mind is at peace, the atmosphere around us becomes heaven. But some people create the devil and hell instead!

DEATH

You often say that practicing zazen is getting into one's coffin. What is death, really, in Zen?

Good question. Zazen and death are not the same. Death means not breathing anymore, while in zazen you concentrate on breathing. No relationship. Have you read the *Genjokoan**? It explains the relationship between zazen and death very precisely. You must read it. You will understand.

Firewood becomes ashes; the ashes cannot become firewood again and the firewood cannot see its own ashes. It's the same relationship as that between life and death.

And yet I say: zazen is the same as getting into one's coffin, living nirvana, like death. Nirvana is the finish of everything—ku, non-*shiki.* * Activity stops. The complete stop means death. The total cessation of the three actions defines death.

But Hinayana* Buddhism is wrong when it says that in order to get to nirvana one must stop eating, stop breathing. Illusions disappear in those conditions, no doubt, but one is almost dead. Buddha tried those methods and discarded them.

Professor Akishige says that "when consciousness ceases the body is close to the state of death." Tranquil. But that is not the normal condition of consciousness either. You grow weak, and a little peculiar. Being close to death is not hishiryo consciousness. For one day, two days, a few days, it is possible to stop eating; during his period of austerity Buddha ate a single grain of rice each day. But I never said that one had to practice the condition of death. Nobody would want to follow that.

Do not be anxious. You must eat, but be able to reduce the amount of food you need. Dogen wrote, "An empty stomach is not the normal condition," because then both body and consciousness become weak. The brain grows tired and a special form of consciousness develops that can lead to hallucinations. I have had the experience myself. The mind takes complete control over the body.

In Zen, trying to achieve some special condition is not the way. True, nirvana is also a balance of mind and body. But eating is necessary.

When I am teaching I say that you should become as though you were getting into your coffin. The words can jar people. It's not necessary to get into a real coffin. *You can imagine it: "nothing."*

This morning you said that the spirit of Master Yamada, who has just died, was in this dojo. What do you think about life after death?

It is a problem with which many people are preoccupied. To cover it thoroughly I should have to give a two-hour lecture.

What happens after death? This is a religious problem, and it is not necessary to think too much about it. People who don't want to die are always worried about it. *In Buddhism you will find no commentary on after-death.* "Here and now" is what is essential. Metaphysical issues cannot be settled one way or the other. Their premises can be neither confirmed nor disproved; nothing can be decided about them.

What does the mind become after death? Nobody has come back to tell us. So we must not be too attached to death. That is the sense of Dogen's famous saying, "The firewood cannot see its ashes." Firewood stands for life and ashes for death.

"The ashes cannot see the firewood."

You can also compare life to the images forming on the television screen, death to the interruption of the images when you turn the set off.

If we look, our vision is a subjective vision. If we turn the button, the image disappears.

But do you think the soul lives on after death?

What do you think?

That is a very complex problem, one that is creating difficulties for modern science. I cannot deny it, but I cannot believe it either. Science cannot find a soul in the brain or heart or in any other part of the body.

And yet the action of our consciousness goes on. Our karma, our actions, the action of our karma continue. If you hit someone the action continues. When we think, the karma of that thought continues. When you turn off your television set the image disappears from the screen but it continues over the waves. It's the same. The world of now and the spiritual world are reversed, become opposite, but continue. It is a problem which is at once easy and hard. But if I explain it, you are likely to misunderstand.

I do not believe that the soul goes up to heaven or down to

hell. It cannot get out of the coffin to go anywhere. But the influence of consciousness goes on.

There is the story of the master and the disciple who were going to a funeral. The disciple pointed to the coffin and said, "Is that living or not?" And the master answered, "I cannot answer, I say nothing!" The master was clever, neither negative nor positive.

To think "I'll go to heaven and be with my family again" is imagination. But to answer "You're a fool to believe that" is no good either. It is better to say nothing.

I have my own ideas, but if I make categories in regard to this matter what I say will be generalization, whereas in reality I should have to give a different answer to each person. The problem is a very deep one, touching upon the essence of religions. You must not make categories; the problem is different for each person.

The principle of reincarnation provides an answer to many of our questions. But Buddhism and Hinduism do not agree on this subject.

It is true that Buddhism was influenced by the old Indian tradition to some degree. But Buddha himself was not so keen on it.

You change your incarnation: that is Buddhism's answer.

In Zen, there is no reincarnation, for example, a cat turning into a human being or vice versa. That is a theory from the Indian tradition, and not a very important one, even if it did influence Mahayana Buddhism. Does the soul remain after death? It's a problem for one's consciousness.

According to modern physiology, the brain and its cells continue to live for two or three days—maybe, in some dead people, consciousness is not completely dead. The last state of consciousness is very important. You continue on from that state of consciousness.

What should be your last thought? If you are accustomed to practicing zazen your last breath will be that of a normal consciousness—without consciousness.

In times past, when physiology was not so highly developed, imagination played an important part in the work of philosophers and religious figures: reincarnation, the resurrection of Christ. In Christianity, there is eschatology, belief about the last day of the world that has not come yet. But at the death of each individual the world stops, and one can communicate with eternity.

If there's no such thing as reincarnation, why is one's last moment of consciousness so important?

The mushotoku attitude is important. "I must go to heaven, I must get born in another life"; you don't need to think like that. If you think of anything, if you have a desire, then you're still hanging on to your past existence. It's better to be mushotoku unconsciously. True calm, true peace.

People tend to attach too much importance to the idea of heaven: "If I die I must go to heaven." It is useless to build such images in your subconscious. Nonconsciousness is the highest attitude. If you have a thought, it will not be effaced during that day or two of transition; but if you are in harmony with the cosmic system your activity, your consciousness will quickly return to the cosmos.

During zazen you can harmonize with the cosmic system. Psychology defines it as nonconsciousness. Buddhism calls it the alaya consciousness; and I am always repeating that you must go back to the normal consciousness. Through zazen you can get there unconsciously; it is the transcendent consciousness, out of which right behavior, right actions can spring. All our cells, all our neurons are activated.

Each thing you perceive is felt by your neurons. Nervous energy is transmitted directly to them. Desires arise from perceptions: the desire to continue, the desire to possess. This activity, the activity of living, is incessant. Ideas are constantly arising, the consciousness grows complicated.

So we must come back and back to the normal condition. Even when we sleep our consciousness is at work, part of the time; when we sleep completely, that is nonconsciousness. Two hours of deep sleep, then dreams start again. It's all very complicated.

In zazen, the body has just the right tonus. When you are asleep you are completely relaxed, no tonus at all. But during zazen you can see the dreams come out of the subconscious and you can return to the state of nonconsciousness, the existence of which has been established by modern physiology and psychology. But you must not say, "Now I have no consciousness!" because that is conscious, and the state I am talking about is not a conscious one.

When I say, "Five minutes more! Concentrate hard!" those last five minutes are very important.

At the beginning many thoughts come, but after a while one can reach this state. Some people reach it at the end of five minutes, by concentrating on their posture and breathing out. You must not slump over or hang your head; you must keep the back of the neck well-stretched. When people think, their thumbs droop. You must pull yourself up and be very vigilant.

So you don't believe in reincarnation?

Believe? It is not so important. It is not necessary to believe. To determine whether reincarnation exists or not is a subjective matter. My own ideas on the subject are not entirely negative, but I do not say that "I must believe in it."

As far as reincarnation is concerned, nobody has come back from death to tell us about it. But it excites the imagination, and primitive religions had a great many ideas about it. In this area, you cannot decide whether one path or the other is the right one. You can believe or not believe. I have had many metaphysical experiences and *I believe in the metaphysical world; but you cannot reduce it to some trivial thing.* The cosmos is infinite. People write about the metaphysical world but they can only touch upon minute aspects of it, whereas it is infinite. So we cannot talk about it. My experience and that of other people are not the same, and we cannot decide if it is this way or that. Making categories reduces things to trivial dimensions.

If somebody can remember his previous lives, doesn't that imply that something is permanent?

People think of their own egos. They want to understand and cannot understand completely. They think egotistically. If you are not egotistical then the subject is not so crucial; zazen is much more important. *Here and now can be far more effective.*

Master Dogen wrote deeply on this question of before birth, after death. Before birth: a drop of sperm from the father, an ovule from the mother . . . a drop of blood . . . That also is ku.

It's not worth thinking about, analyzing. Only here and now is important. When you have to die you have to die, and in that moment this life ends.

The more egotistical people are, the more they are attached to life and the more they think about death.

Where did Bodhidharma go when he died?

He's not here and it doesn't matter. Do not think about where you will go after your death. Think only about here and now. When you die you will go into a coffin, unless you die at sea; they don't use coffins there.

Here-now is important. If you concentrate on each point here and now, the points will become a line and unconsciously, naturally, automatically, you will go to your coffin and sleep in the ground. It's like zazen. Now I must die and I concentrate on zazen.

The relationship is the same as between firewood and ash. The wood does not know, cannot look at its ashes. The wood can look at the ashes of another log but not at its own. Your eyes cannot see your own eyes, except in a mirror. It's the same thing as between life and death, the burned wood that becomes ash. Ash cannot think that before it was wood, and vice versa.

You cannot look at your death. It is a very difficult, subjective problem. I can look at your death but you can't. Once you are dead, your death cannot look at your life. It is a subjective problem which you are thinking about now as though it were an objective problem. The object is not important, only the subject. It's also a problem of time. "Here and now" includes eternity. Don't make categories.

The question is more difficult than some factual issue that can be solved by science and about which everybody can agree. The subjective aspect is more profound. It is yourself that you are studying. Nobody understands except you. In regard to deep problems everybody has a different opinion. So it is difficult to help you. The subjective problem of each person is different and science cannot solve it. If I want to help you I must become you!

Through zazen you can sever the karma of body, speech, and mind. Through death too. Is death the same as satori?

Yes, exactly. The word nirvana means death. Nirvana is the perfect satori. Sometimes it refers to the death of Buddha, perfect extinction. Once we are dead our karma stops creating, no more karma of body, mouth, thought.

But there are two doctrines: one says that everything is finished and the other says that karma continues. To you that seems contradictory.

In zazen we can make our karma decrease, not stop it. The mouth is shut, the body's karma stops, but that of the brain cannot stop completely, it's too difficult—or else, after a minute or two, you go to sleep. That is because karma is manifested first in the subconscious and appears as a dream.

It is really extremely difficult to stop the karma of consciousness. In fact, it is eternal and continues after death. Body and mind are total unity, so if the body comes to an end and dies the consciousness also ceases living. *What is life?* At death, what stops is the physical activity of the body. But the mind is not separate from it.

In Zen there are no commentaries on the problem of substance or on metaphysical questions. And yet they raise many difficulties, I know. Such as, if the body dies, does the mind die too? Many religions claim that the soul flies away. There are scientists who think the same thing: they say the mind floats around for a year or two. Some people imagine that the mind enters into the body of a newborn child. Others say the soul goes to hell or to heaven. Shakyamuni* Buddha never said anything of the sort.

But the influence of karma continues. The elements that compose the body remain after death, after cremation. The water and blood go into air and earth. The elements remain. Only their physical aspect changes. There is only a physical transformation, and since matter and spirit are unity there is something that remains and is eternally reincarnated. It is possible to think like this.

Even the body is not completely finished after death, so our life is like a bubble on the surface of the water, on the surface of the cosmic order. It appears and floats on the horizon, seventy years, eighty years, sometimes one hundred years, then it bursts and disappears—but in reality it continues. There are big bubbles and little bubbles.

But you must not be thinking about it all the time, for it tires the brain. Better to concentrate on zazen. Of course, it's interesting to think about it, and karma is important. "How can I avoid a bad reincarnation?" All the great religions worry about the question.

It is not accurate to deny, but to affirm raises a difficult metaphysical problem. It's better to remain in hishiryo consciousness.

So the most important thing is to keep concentrating here and now?

That is faith, the king of samadhi,* *of concentration.*

Past karma comes to an end. It appears and reappears, you must let it pass by. During zazen, too, karma rises up as in dreams, good and bad dreams. You must let them pass by. The karma of consciousness is the most subtle. Those of the body, of activity, of speech are easier to deal with because they are also governed by laws and the presence of other people, so it is easier to correct them.

Religious life is reflection. If you practice zazen you can decrease your karma unconsciously, automatically, naturally, and reflect.

We cannot sever everything. But if, for example, instead of coming to this sesshin you had gone to the Club Métditerranée you might have created more bad karma, whereas in zazen, on the contrary, you can very exactly decrease it. *True faith, the religious life, is reflection, observation, concentration.*

We must be mushotoku. I keep saying that. If you respect the *kai,* * the precepts, and if you are mushotoku, your karma will decrease automatically. If we observe it we can make it diminish.

The karma of speech: do not lie. That of the body too. Through zazen our daily lives can continue our reflection and it develops. We can have a better life and perhaps the mistakes we make will not be as big as the ones we made before. Some people go on making them, but that is the result of their karma, not of zazen. Some people have so bad a karma that they can't manage to follow my teaching. But those who continue practicing zazen can find their underlying truth.

This morning you said one can have the experience of death in zazen. What is it?

Forgetting everything. You abandon your ego the way you abandon your body when you get into your coffin. If you die, no more anything.

And why do you call that awakening?

You must embrace contradictions. Westerners always want to make categories! I taught you today: sometimes conquer, sometimes abandon. Both are very important. *Waking up doesn't just mean opening your eyes: dying is also waking up.* You must lean neither to the right nor to the left.

How can you live here and now when you are always thinking about death?

Life and death are identical.

If you accept death here and now your life will be more profound. You must not be attached to life. Or to death.

When it is time to die you die and return to the cosmos.

When our activity comes to an end, when our life is finished, then we must die. You must understand death.

Who understands?

Only the true ego understands.

Why do you talk about eternity after death and not before birth?

Because human beings are like that. Most people don't understand. If you solve this problem here and now your life will be peaceful and you will be very happy.

Why are we born?

Because your father and mother gave birth to you. You have raised a great problem, a real koan. Think about it.

"Why was I born? To feed myself? To love? To acquire knowledge?" That question is the object of our life. And what do other people think? Each person has a different opinion. Some say, to perfect our life or mankind; others say, to enable consciousness to be incarnated or in order that cosmic life can be lived individually. Each of these replies is correct. This is the question on which all religions are based.

Buddha, discovering zazen, solved the problem of birth and death.

Zen to bun mei, Zen and civilization

ZEN AND THE WEST

MODERN CIVILIZATION

Isn't Zen becoming a fad?

What does that matter? A fad is a response to a need but it does not last. To endure, a practice demands effort and perseverance. There are always people who understand and continue, beyond passing fads and fashions. The fad leaves something behind. The wave ebbs but the ocean remains.

Why did you come to Europe?

Because I wanted to! I'm very glad I did.

I like France and Europe very much, so I came. That's an easy question, and an easy answer. Here's another:

I came here to teach true Zen to Europeans, because they do not understand it. Intellectuals have only a literary notion of it. My master said to me, "It would be best to go to Europe. Bodhidharma brought Zen from India to China, Dogen brought it from China to Japan, and from Japan it must go to Europe. It's very important."

When the soil is exhausted the seed can no longer grow. But if you change the soil a good seed can develop. Europe is fresh, as far as Zen is concerned, and I hope that the seed of Zen will grow there. Now the Japanese are trying to imitate European Zen. So it is being effective in both directions!

Zen does not seem to be made for a mass public; why do you use television and the press?

In our age the media are important. Information must be transmitted by whatever means are available. Why use them only for superficial things, why hide a profound teaching? Everyone today is looking for a meaning in life. Everyone has a right to wake up. The religious person must jump into the water and learn how to swim well enough to help those who are drowning.

Zen has been influenced by the cultures of India, China, and Japan. Are there elements in our culture that can influence it; in other words, will Zen take anything from the West?

Bodhidharma, coming from India, gave Zen to China. China was strongly marked by it. The country was already highly developed; when the Chinese civilization accepted Zen (Ch'an) its own philosophy was deeply influenced, whereas Indian Zen, for its part, gained great vigor from its contact with Chinese naturalism and pragmatism.

Then Master Dogen took Zen to Japan, where it had a powerful influence on the spirit of the samurai and on culture in general. Japanese civilization still bears the marks of it today.

More than ten years ago, I brought Zen to Europe. The civilization here is growing weak now, and whenever a civilization grows weak Zen gives it renewed vitality. In China, too, there was an overdeveloped intellectual culture and Zen revived it. In Japan, in Dogen's day, traditional Buddhism had become almost wholly esoteric.

What weakens people is too much use of the imagination and intellect. So Dogen restored the balance with Zen. There must not be only spirituality and imagination; there must be practice as well.

Zen is easy to practice, but it is hard too. The posture is simple, yet some aspects of it are difficult and require the highest mastery.

Civilization in Europe today is decadent, and not only in Europe but throughout the scientific West. If you practice zazen, however, Western civilization will certainly grow strong again. I believe that.

It will be the same as for the Chinese civilization in Bodhidharma's day.

People in the West have good brains. If you practice zazen

you will become more active and balanced, and Western civilization will continue to be powerful in the centuries to come.

But isn't practicing zazen a way of escaping from the economy, society, the world?

No, I don't believe that.

A newborn child is attracted by food, by its mother's breast. An adolescent is intensely aware of sexuality. Adults are drawn to money and possessions. And then come honors. But when human beings find that none of these are enough to bring the happiness they want, then they turn toward spirituality. That is not running away; on the contrary, it is proof of realism, evolution. *Only human beings have access to the spiritual realm.*

How can a busy career be reconciled with the practice of Zen?

It is just because your life is so busy that the practice of Zen will be so good for it. You will do what you have to do much better because you will be concentrated, and you may also rid yourself of a mass of useless things. You will see your everyday life with new eyes. One koan says, "*When mind is free everything around is free.*"

What would the world be like if everybody were a Zen monk?

It is not necessary to become a monk: I have never denied the importance of work and everyday life.

Everyone should be able to earn his food. "Here and now" is important!

In this dojo we do not practice zazen twenty-four hours a day; even I am not always practicing zazen. Through practice, zazen becomes the support of your everyday life; through zazen your entire life becomes Zen.

So it is not necessary to become a monk; but if you want to, you will have a life beyond ordinary human life, you will have the highest spiritual life.

What is spiritual life? Knowing oneself. Every great human has said it, they have all understood: "I am absolute Nothing . . . "

When we realize that we have no ego, that ego or self is

nothing but interdependence, that we are exactly and no more than the result of the influence of our environment, that in all this there is no room for a me, that our life is without permanent substance—then we are open to the dimensions of the cosmos, we can receive its energy and we can create.

Open your hands and you will receive everything, even material things. *Don't be afraid; that is satori.*

How do you see the world situation in terms of human evolution?

Some things are not developing; on the contrary, they are regressing. This is a major problem of civilization. Some people believe that civilization means progress, others think that it is the opposite. Who is wrong, who is right? Are humans going forward or backward?

If the central brain and hypothalamus are both growing weak, then that is not evolution; or if the inner brain becomes weaker and the outer brain stronger. [In speaking about the brain, Deshimaru Roshi uses "inner," "central," "old," "primitive" as synonyms and "outer," "forebrain," "hypothalamus" also.] What is indispensable is harmony and balance between the two. When the inner brain and hypothalamus both grow strong, then there is true evolution. That is why zazen is important. I am always talking about balance. If there is no balance between the inner, primitive brain and the outer, intellectual brain, there is weakness. *How do we harmonize the two?*

That raises the problem of human education. It should be changed. Here in this dojo you receive a good education, a true education.

Why are we imperfect? Were we perfect once and are we supposed to become that way again?

That is the whole problem of civilization. Which is better, the old civilization or modern civilization? *It's a false problem, because we cannot know the answer.*

In the beginning the inner brain was highly developed; with civilization the outer envelope has grown larger. As the outside grows, the inside atrophies, the two are out of balance, the nerves are out of balance, and we see mental illness and neuroses and madness, as in the case of Nietzche and many philosophers. Modern education addresses itself solely to the outer brain. How can we strengthen the inner brain?

I have seen the cave paintings of Lascaux and Tassili. Thousands of years ago, in those caves, men made drawings, paintings, that are beautiful and delicate. I like them better than Picasso's. Human evolution is a great problem. Our intelligence has increased enormously since the Middle Ages, but where is wisdom? What is evolution today? Our muscles are growing weak and our brains too. People are not progressing, even though their intelligence and knowledge are progressing.

The West must grow strong. Its religion is not the same as in Asia and Africa, but I hope they will merge together. The Africans are combative; that is the characteristic of the desert, and religion is strong there. The Mohammedans fight and organize. Orientals are calmer; that comes from the influence of the monsoons, the rains that lay everything to waste so that people have no choice but to be patient. Buddha did not like fighting. He wanted peace. So Buddhism grew and influenced the whole of Asia.

What is the way to find true peace for the whole of mankind? Our environment is buffeted by political problems. We need to take in the beneficial waves and refuse the harmful ones. That is why effort is important, too, a new effort, a new type of effort. Europeans do not make enough effort, they tire quickly. That is also why practicing zazen is important. If you practice zazen you can make an effort. I think that even in Africa not many young people are capable of great effort. They're strong but not strongly motivated. What must we do in order to be able to make an effort? *What is the relationship between activity and aggressiveness?* If you are very active you need to get rid of your energy and if you use it to do harm it becomes aggressiveness, which is not good. If a person becomes aggressive you should counter with wisdom. I have never said that people should be aggressive. They should practice wisdom and create true activity. We need to create balance; wisdom without any activity to express it leads to bestiality. It is important that we do not behave like animals, but also that we are not just spiritual, like ghosts. Only balance matters, only that is the direction of evolution.

We are living in an age of total decadence. Do you believe that civilization will be able to put itself right?

Yes, I believe it will go straight, and in the end people will get better; what is bad will be transformed. Everything is extremely difficult right now all over the world, but afterwards, certainly it will change. Another civilization will be born.

EVERYDAY LIFE

What should people do in their everyday lives?

Work, go to the toilet, eat; whatever you like!

If you practice zazen regularly you get into the habit of it; as far as I personally am concerned, for example, my brain works the same way in everyday life as it does during zazen.

Zazen early in the morning influences the rest of your day and you learn to react to everything that happens with the same steady frame of mind. When people leave the dojo after morning zazen they are calm, and this carries over into their life outside; their minds are clear, tranquil, not at all tired . . . it's very effective. That's one reason why people like to practice.

It's not good to have your head hanging down all the time; so remember to stretch your neck and pull in your chin. Everybody nowadays has their head hanging down or sticking out in front of them. The neck should be pulled up all the way along, so that the brain can be irrigated by the blood and become clear.

How do you reconcile the idea of "no-gain" with zazen in everyday life?

If, during zazen, you have no goal and are not hoping to get something, you are mushotoku. If you gain something without wanting it, that's good. You don't have to refuse it. But you must not try for it. During zazen you must not want to grasp something —illumination, satori, good health, calm nerves, no more anxiety, progress in Zen. It is not necessary to think that way. Just follow my teaching: concentrate on posture and breathing. That is enough.

To have a goal, not just in zazen but in everyday living, to want to get something or grasp something, *is a sickness of the mind.*

> *Yes, but sometimes the very fact that you don't have a goal can be a problem.*

You don't need a goal if, here and now, you are concentrating on what you are doing: on your work when you're working, on your food when you're eating, on going to the toilet when you're on the toilet. When you speak, just speak, and say only what is important in that particular situation.

Here and now, if you are concentrated, your concentration will follow you to your death and illuminate you unfailingly; but that is not having a goal.

On the other hand, *you must have an ideal,* that is necessary. But an ideal and a goal are completely different. The greatest ideal is universal love, not selfish love. Universal love is not a goal, it's an ideal.

Hope is necessary too. What is hope? Do you hope to become a clever politician? Not so good. A great artist? Maybe. But what is a great ideal? Action without any thought of profit, mushotoku. That is the greatest ideal.

It's useless to long for money or honors. Only concentrate here and now. That is Zen.

> *But sometimes one has to think about commitments one has made or plans for the future?*

When one thinks, one thinks. *One thinks here and now, makes plans here and now, remembers here and now.* When I write my autobiography I think about the past. When I have to make plans I think about the future. The succession of here-and-now's becomes cosmic and stretches into infinity.

> *But if you practice mushotoku, how can you make plans and have desires?*

Everyday life and zazen are not the same. In everyday life you must gain; a businessman has to concentrate in order to make a profit.

I am talking about the inner spirit, the subjective aspect. When you are mushotoku, even if you lose you are always free.

In everyday life you need wisdom. You must use your wisdom. At the same time, it is necessary to be mushotoku in your dealings with everyone. But the minds of most people are never mushotoku; they think, "If I give him this maybe he'll give me that in return." It's a problem of the spirit, the mind.

You said that the true attitude of mind consists in not choosing, but in everyday life you have to make choices all the time. How can you reconcile the two?

That's the same as confusing metaphysical and physical problems.

In searching for the Way, do not choose; in everyday life, choose.

There can be no choice in seeking the Way, apprehending truth. In everyday life, on the other hand, what counts is making choices. But it is bad to be attached to one's choices, to limit them. You must choose but remain free to choose, and free in the result of your choice.

I don't choose my disciples; some stay, some go away. My mind is at peace; it does not choose.

Karma determines your decisions, but the cosmic order is not so precise: sometimes a misfortune produces good fortune, sometimes happiness leads to misery. But the spirit, the mind stays the same: calm and peaceful. Satori.

In practical life wisdom is necessary. An object that is too intensely desired cannot be attained because the mind is attached to the desire, and the person suffers or goes mad. All things come to the person whose mind is peaceful and filled with wisdom.

Wisdom means learning not to suffer from a failure, and learning to reduce one's desires. Return to the normal condition.

What should we do to live zazen in everyday life?

You should concentrate on each act of everyday life: when you're in bed with your wife, concentrate on her. If you think about zazen just then, it's no good. Harmonize with your family; then it will follow and harmonize with you!

If you feel like losing your temper, if you are carried away by your emotions, then breathe deeply as in zazen: that will be much more effective.

You say that paying attention to posture and breathing is satori. Can't a person concentrate the same way in everyday life?

When you are paying attention to your everyday concerns, yes, you can remain concentrated. It's the same as zazen, whether you're going to the toilet or eating or working.

If you're used to concentrating during zazen you can achieve the same concentrated mind in all your actions, unconsciously, naturally, automatically. In the beginning, of course, you need to use your will, but it is not easy to achieve concentration by willpower alone: you have to keep thinking about it all the time. If you practice zazen you form the habit of being concentrated, and you can be concentrated whatever the subject or activity. And if you keep on practicing you will concentrate without having to use any willpower at all.

How can a conscious effort in everyday life provide a natural, spontaneous result?

Body and mind are not separate. If you have to pay attention, the body concentrates and the consciousness too. Both work at the same time. If you concentrate on the mind the body changes too. If the body is not concentrated it goes limp and so does the attitude of mind. If the body concentrates so does the mind. There is not just one side.

If you are on a road you think, "I must pay attention to the cars." Your body and mind both concentrate.

If you think about your posture during zazen you will remain concentrated, and I can see your concentration; but if you are overconcentrated that is not good either.

It's the same in everyday life, eating, walking, going to the toilet. At every moment of your life if your posture is bad the mind or spirit becomes bad as well, and the other way round.

We live in a world of fear. How can one deal with that?

There are many kinds of fear. Fear of failing an examination, for instance. But *you should not be attached to that fear;* it's better to let go of the idea of passing the exam, then you won't be afraid anymore.

People are afraid because they are attached to their egos. Fear, apprehension have to do with attachment.

It's better to avoid fear. Just concentrate here and now. Fear comes from doubt, anxiety. Don't be too attached to danger and don't come too close to it. Sometimes it's better to run away. Courting danger is stupid. We should feel inside our body if an accident is about to happen. If there is too much noise and excitement it's better to stay quietly in your place. Don't go to dangerous places. Of course, that doesn't hold for people who love adventure.

But in living our lives there is no need to be afraid.

If we ruminate and think and doubt then we'll be even more afraid. Concentrate on breathing out. Then the brain will return to its normal condition. You must not be egotistical. When you let go of your ego you stop being afraid. If you're always concentrated you'll be strong. But even so, do not stray too close to the demon of danger.

I'd like to know what you think of the macrobiotic diet?

Its chief value is in healing illnesses. It is a therapeutic technique, not a philosophy or a religion.

I myself follow a macrobiotic diet sometimes, for my health. But it's not necessary, especially for young people. If you eat like a pigeon when you're young your stomach will be weak; meat and alcohol are necessary sometimes. But if you eat and drink too much then the macrobiotic diet becomes necessary.

But that is not Zen. Zazen is true, profound religion. If you practice zazen you can understand what is going on in your body and choose the kind of diet you need. Through zazen you can understand, and then regulate accordingly.

People who follow such diets tend to attach too much importance to their bodies and the choice of their food, and in the end they fall ill. Too much attachment to health leads to egotism. Unconscious egotism, but egotism all the same. It is important to pay attention to your health, but worrying about it all the time weakens the mind. I know lots of macrobiotic people, and they lack compassion, they are selfish. That is why Shakyamuni Buddha abandoned asceticism; it destroys one's harmony with other people.

If you refuse everything when you are with other people, you cannot harmonize. I don't care for meat but when people offer it to me I must accept. It is extremely important to harmonize. I am a monk so I have to educate people, teach them what to do. A monk has a duty to observe the precepts but that is only one side, so I look at each person, and my teaching differs for each person. To those who have a narrow mind I say, "You must drink whiskey," or I tell them to get themselves a gigolo, while to another person I would say, "No more alcohol; get rid of your gigolo."

Is there fasting in Zen?

Yes, but it's not necessary for people in good health. It cleans the body, it's useful sometimes. It is good to fast once a year or once a month. I did when I was younger. It is also good to eat less sometimes, and it is less of a hardship to moderate what one eats than to stop eating altogether.

You must not be obsessed by questions of what you eat and drink or don't eat and drink. It is hard for young people to restrict themselves, and no diet should be continued for too long.

You should eat everything; then your mind becomes broad and generous. But at the same time you should control, have a little of each thing and not too much of any.

What do you think about the education of children?

An important and difficult question. It's like a kite: *sometimes you have to pull on the string, sometimes you have to let it pull you.* If you pull too hard it falls down; if you don't pull hard enough it falls down too.

Modern children are spoiled, wasted. Parents must regulate their severity and their indulgence, strike a balance.

If a mother has the strength to do that, the child will have it too. Educating the mother is most important. If she makes mistakes the child makes mistakes. Honesty is necessary too: the child must be able to see into its mother's mind. If she makes a mistake she must excuse herself to the child.

ZEN AND CHRISTIANITY

Are other religions compatible with Zen?

Of course. Zen is beyond religion. Christians, nuns and priests, practice zazen.

What are the main differences between Christianity and Buddhism?

If you think differences exist, they exist. If you think there are no differences, there are none. The source is the same; but people are always trying to set up categories.

When you look at them from the outside they're completely different. But in their deepest spirit I find no difference. They are interdependent. Buddhism has had a strong influence on some Christian theologians and vice versa: there are priests and pastors who have influenced Buddhism. Both influences have been profound. In essence, it comes down to one and the same religion.

Father Lassalle never lectures on Christianity; he talks about Zen. Lots of other Christians do the same. Sometimes I talk about Christianity in my lectures; sometimes I forget Buddha and talk only about God and Christ. According to some authors, the founders of Buddhism, Christianity, Islam, Judaism, and Taoism were five great Initiates. So you must understand the roots. Zen means trying to understand the roots of all religions. Everything else is decoration.

Zen is pure experience and cannot be simply identified with Buddhism, even though it developed within Buddhism. Thus far the "philosophy" which has tried to express something of its meaning (since we have to talk a little, even if words are not so good) has done so in a Buddhist context. Do you believe that if Christians practice Zen they can come one day to express something about it in a form that can be "philosophically" different, in any significant way, from the Buddhist form—for example, in regard to such matters as the interpretation of the relationship between life here and after death, or the relationship between God the Creator and the essence of things?

Zen is not philosophy, not psychology, not doctrine. It is beyond philosophies, concepts, forms. The essence of Zen is not expressed in words. Of course, there is the Zen Buddhism which is a traditional framework with disciplines, rites, and rules. And there is the Zen that is open to everybody, in its teaching of the universality of consciousness, in the practice of meditation, in the perfect posture of zazen. And also in the means it offers, of cultivating one's presence to oneself as an art of living here and now, in the perfection of the instant; and of learning how to release and master the energies within us and by so doing to participate fully in the creation that takes place through us and by our activity every day.

Philosophy comes after practice.

But it is important to attach Zen to its origins and learn them well: its source in India, then Ch'an in China, and then the lineage of all the masters to the present day. Otherwise one could be spreading anything, not true Zen.

If you are faithful in practice, Zen becomes continuous creation.

Through a profound knowledge of the spirit and the source, Westerners will be able in turn to create an original Zen, their own.

How should one talk about God?

In our modern civilization people need some scientific justification if they are going to believe in a Supreme Being. There are too many buddhas, gods. People no longer realize what the words represent. For committed Christians they evoke something, as they do for committed Buddhists, although ultimately, in Buddhism, union with Buddha is not a goal and we speak of ku, void, emptiness. It is more scientific.

In Europe what I say on this point seems simple, because God is the absolute. But in Japan and the Far East there are so many Buddhist sects, so many religions, it all becomes highly complicated because there are so many categories.

In Japan, when a person dies, we say the person becomes Buddha, so the word Buddha has a connotation of death. Young people cannot understand.

What is the difference between the Passion of Christ and the Compassion of Buddha?

Christ opposed the government of his day. A true man of religion should oppose bad policy. He sacrifices himself for others. If Christ had not been crucified Christianity would not have developed; that's why the Cross is important. Afterward, the apostles spread and organized his teaching and cultivated a spirit of compassion in regard to his cruel death. Christ's death created the force of their mission. For Christ and for Buddha, universal love is important. Compassion means love and understanding of the other's mind: if someone is suffering one must feel "sympathy" with that person. Most people are envious, though, which is the opposite of compassion. If somebody is happy or successful we are happy with him; if he is sad, so are we.

At bottom, passion and compassion are not different. Buddha was old, he felt compassion; Christ was young and what he lived was a passion. Christ had less experience of life; that is the only difference.

When you read the Bible it is all very moral. When young people read the sutras they find many contradictions in them because they include so many things, left side, right side.

Christ is beauty, purity, emotion; the moralizing side of Christianity is very tough, very strong. In Buddhism it is, too, but in the end all illusions become satori.

Buddha had many experiences, palace life, lots of women, then six years of mortification. In the end he was half dead. Under the Bodhi tree he was tempted and harassed by all kinds of inner demons. When there was nothing left of him but the skin on his bones Sujata took care of him and gave him milk every day; thanks to this woman, little by little, Buddha recovered his love for real life, his body returned to its normal condition and his mind too: satori.

Balance is important. Too much pleasure and too much self-denial are both bad.

After experiencing true life and true freedom he founded Buddhism, and Buddhism did not agree with the traditional religions, which were too ascetic or moralistic in those days.

The kai, the precepts, came later; and when Hinayana Buddhism became too formalistic Mahayana Buddhism created a new wisdom, which also became too deeply entrenched in tradition in the end. Religions must always be alive, they must not create categories that make the brain narrow and complicated. *Religion is not science, it does not need categories.*

Saint Paul said the whole of creation is suffering and awaiting redemption. What does that mean from the viewpoint of compassion?

Tibetan Buddhism is always talking about compassion, but wisdom is necessary too. One without the other cannot be genuine. You must know how to combine compassion with wisdom.

A father and mother need compassion in bringing up their child, and wisdom, too, which teaches them how to measure out severity and gentleness, tenderness. I like the example of the kite: to make it fly properly you must not curb it too sharply and you must not let it have too much slack. Balance is important.

Buddha's compassion is for all people and does not distinguish between rich and poor. It does not have to do with solving political problems and wars. Religion saves people on a higher plane. *The problem is to change people's minds.*

What I am talking about is not a political revolution but a revolution inside our mind. If people do not change inside themselves, nothing can change. The crisis in our civilization now is caused by the fact that most people's minds are not normal. If the mind changes, civilization changes. Changing minds could solve the problem of oil shortages. People would attend sesshins instead of watching television.

Your behavior influences the behavior of other people.

Last year I was at Eihei-ji, and at the end of a long conversation a Zen monk said to me, "In Zen, when you have satori, you can say, 'I am God!'" Can such a shocking statement be interpreted as being like Saint Paul when he said, "It is not I who lives but Christ who lives in me"?

Zazen is the same thing as God or Buddha. Dogen, the master of transmission, said, "Zazen itself is God." By that he meant that during zazen you are in harmony with the cosmos.

In hishiryo consciousness there is no more anything. It is satori consciousness. The self has dropped away and dissolved. It is the consciousness of God. It is God.

People have a personal God. We are not separate. There is no duality between God, Buddha, and ourselves.

If I say, "I am God or Buddha," I am a little bit crazy. Mushotoku is important. If you think consciously about God or Buddha it's not good. If I say you are God or Buddha while you are practicing zazen it's not at all the same thing as if you say it about yourself. In Zen, you must have no goal.

In hishiryo consciousness the personal self, however illuminated it may be, is still here. Meister Eckhart said, "If you empty yourself God enters into you."

In Zen the ego enters into God. God enters into the ego. Both.

I believe that Zen meditation leads to a deeper knowledge of the self, through the body, through proper posture, through a perception of the body that gives an awareness of belonging to the cosmos. But for me that is not cosmic consciousness. It is the consciousness of being, through my body, a participant in the cosmos. I don't believe the cosmos itself has a specific consciousness.

It is impossible to experience it consciously. That is why the masters use parables or poems or paintings. In Chinese philosophy, the earth and myself have the same root. If we keep saying "God, God, God" nowadays, people don't understand what we are talking about and cannot believe. In Buddhism it is the same with Buddha.

But where is God? We cannot see. The cosmic system, the cosmic consciousness: that we can understand. It exists physically, it is energy. Today science is trying to figure out what cosmic energy is.

We receive that energy in ourselves, by breathing, eating, through our skin. But that isn't all. We also have an ego, a personal consciousness, and that consciousness also receives energy from the cosmos.

Physiologists have studied the question and confirmed this. If our individual consciousness, our ego, is too strong we receive the energy badly. That is why we must abandon our personal consciousness in order to receive God. If we go inside ourselves through concentration, we become receptive. During zazen, in the course of a sesshin, the individual consciousness is purified by meditation and the neurons grow calm. Then we can receive cosmic energy fully.

I also believe that the consciousness is emptied of its habitual impressions, of all the events that strike and touch us, and reaches a deeper level of consciousness, which is the sense of belonging to something larger than oneself, to the cosmic order.

By virtue of that emptiness we can receive the cosmic energy easily because we do not live only by ourselves. The cosmic order guides and directs us. Our autonomic nerves, for example, are not operated by our own will. They are directed by cosmic life. In your religion you say, "God disposes." We are not alone; our lives are disposed by God, by Buddha, by the manifestation of energy.

Perhaps what is behind my hesitation is the expression "cosmic consciousness." Teilhard de Chardin talked about a "cosmic sense"; when we go down into ourselves we feel that we belong to the cosmos. Isn't that the same as attributing a consciousness to the cosmos itself?

Consciousness coincides with life. Japanese doctors say, "Everything has a consciousness, everything is consciousness." Even plants have a consciousness; if you stretch out your arm to wrench a flower off its stem, it shrinks away. Science is doing research in this field.

Each existence has a consciousness. *In the end, things are hard to explain, and that's why we say "God."* I am very concerned with the question right now because in Zen we must always find an explanation and be realistic. So sometimes Zen denies Buddha.

What is the cosmic system? What is cosmic truth? In the end we say "God" or "Buddha." That is the ultimate term. If people believe in God or in Buddha the level of their understanding is more profound. But we must not make categories, and so I try to explain both scientifically and sometimes through poetry. Do not make categories. If you do, that is not the true God, the true Buddha.

I say that our consciousness is swifter than the cosmos. That means that God is greater than the cosmos. In Buddhism, ku, the void, is greater than the cosmos.

sho go, satori or awakening

AWAKENING

CONSCIOUSNESS

What is the difference between subconscious and unconscious?

In Buddhism there are six forms of consciousness: alaya, *manas,** and so forth. Manas consciousness corresponds more or less to Jung's collective unconscious. But Jung did not practice zazen so he did not know hishiryo consciousness. From his own experience all he knew was the consciousness of the forebrain and maybe something of the primitive brain, so he was not able to get very far. He was unable to practice a true meditation and could study other kinds only as objects. And in the end, it all turned into nothing but thoughts.

Rinzai Zen and the collective unconscious have a good deal in common. Nietzsche went mad. Van Gogh too . . . They were looking too hard for purity, the absolute, God, true truth, and in the end they went mad. The same thing can happen by concentrating too hard on koans in Rinzai, except that there you have a master who guides you and keeps you from making mistakes. If you have a true master to guide you, you can understand, and wake up.

The master says to the disciple, "Leave this room! No, no, not by the door!" So the disciple turns to the window. "No, not by the window!" "Then where?" "Just leave!" You cannot leave through this exit or through that, not by the summit or by the base, not by the south or by the west. And so the master awakens the disciple's understanding.

But with philosophy it is very difficult. Sometimes philosophers go mad in the end because they use only their forebrain. But we can also think with the body, think infinitely . . . But you must not make categories!

It is written in the *Shodoka** that it is not necessary to seek truth or sever illusions. I am always saying during zazen, "*Do not run after anything and do not run away from illusions.*" It is not necessary to say to oneself "I must not think," because that's still thinking. You must be natural, let the subconscious arise . . . But one time, you have to let go, let yourself drop completely, as though to the bottom of the sea, then rise to the surface again and float.

Neurotic people are always anxious. They're like somebody who doesn't know how to swim and falls into the water. They start to sink, become frightened and say, "I must not sink, I must not sink," they swallow more and more water . . . and in the end they drown. But if they let go of their thoughts and let themselves go down to the bottom, their body will come back to the surface naturally . . . That's Zen.

If you are in pain during zazen you must continue, keep straight, to the end. If you are in pain you can abandon your ego and experience satori unconsciously, naturally, automatically . . .

> *I don't understand what you mean by going down to the bottom.*

When you're in the water and sinking, when you let go of any thought of life and death, let go of your ego completely, then your being concentrates solely on breathing out and you come to the surface. It's the same state of mind as in zazen.

A monk on a ship was caught in a great storm and in his panic, instinctively, he began zazen, accepting death, accepting that he was about to go to the bottom of the ocean. Concentrating naturally on breathing out, he let himself sink, and he rose naturally back to the surface, and that went on until he floated to shore, just breathing in and breathing out.

Another man had an epileptic fit as he was crossing a stream, and he fell off the bridge into the water. Later, he woke up lying on the bank. He realized that the fit that had caused him to fall had also saved him by making it impossible for him to feel the fear of drowning.

When I wake up I always remember my dreams. Should I attach importance to that or not?

You remember your dreams because your brain is tired. Everybody dreams. The body sleeps but the mind is still awake and it dreams. If your brain is healthy you forget your dreams when you wake up. In half-sleep you also have dreams and their imprint remains when you wake. Some people try to run after their dreams and that makes them feel tired when they get up. You should forget, let them pass by, not run after the recollection of a dream.

Does it change anything to analyze dreams?

That is not necessary.

Do you mean that dreams have no value?

They make you complicated. The strong sensations and impressions of everyday life come back, the karma of your brain, the jolts recorded by your neurons. Zazen also brings out your subconscious and your illusions, but in very different conditions.

When you dream you don't know you are dreaming. For example, there is the famous Zen story of a man who was dreaming that he was walking down the street on a winter evening. Suddenly he sees a pouch full of coins on the ground. He tries to take hold of it but it's stuck fast in the ice. What to do? He urinates on the ice to melt it and grabs the pouch with both hands. But oooh, ow, it hurts, what's happened? The man wakes up: instead of a starry sky he sees the ceiling of his bedroom, his testicles are clutched in his hand and aching painfully, and the bed is soaked!

That was the only thing real in the dream . . . When we dream we don't know where reality is any longer. During zazen it's easy to know where it is. You can see your illusions and your karma objectively. In dreams everything comes pell-mell: terrors, shocks, the past, impressions. During zazen you can contemplate whatever comes up from the subconscious as in a mirror, recognize that this or that desire is not so important . . . You are no longer afraid and can observe yourself. It's not the same as in dreams. You shouldn't be attached to the memory of dreams. And in zazen you shouldn't be attached to thoughts or run after illusions, but rather let them go by. The germ of one thought arises, another one follows . . . let them pass by.

After zazen one's brain feels clear and rested. Dreams do the same thing but it's not necessary to try to remember them. Better to forget them.

What do you think about premonitory dreams?

They're part of the metaphysical world. We cannot deny our relationship with that world. If you have faith, you can communicate with the metaphysical world. If your thought concentrates strongly on certain objects, it will create seeds of karma in the neurons and as a result will influence you yourself and your environment.

What about magic powers?

Magic powers are not so difficult to acquire. But in Zen no importance is attached to them. In some religions people are always trying to acquire magic powers but those are not true religions.

Magic powers can be used on certain special occasions. I can use them. But it is not the object of Zen to obtain anything at all . . .

If you carry your practice of zazen to extremes, day and night in a cave in the mountains without eating, and drinking nothing but water for months on end, you will certainly acquire magic powers. But they do not last. The moment you drink a glass of saki they vanish away . . .

To want to acquire magic powers is an egotistical desire, trivial, and ultimately of no importance. It's no different from wanting to become a prestidigitator or a circus artist. Religion is not a circus.

One often has involuntary thoughts during zazen; one wants not to think about something but it keeps coming back.

That is the subconscious, or the collective unconscious. It is like a dream, an illusion. During zazen you don't use your forebrain, but you shouldn't try to prevent unconscious thoughts from arising, because the thalamus becomes active automatically. Jung said that if one could devise a means of revealing the unconscious it would be a momentous discovery. With zazen it is possible . . .

Psychoanalysts are always looking at dreams. *But during zazen you can become completely intimate with yourself, see and know yourself objectively.*

What is natural consciousness, body consciousness?

Bio-consciousness. I call it body consciousness, the scientists say bio-consciousness. It is what explains the fact that we can think with the body. Ordinarily people use only the left side of their brains to think with; but if you concentrate hard enough on your posture and breathing, the entire body can begin to think.

According to Dr. Paul Chauchard every cell has a soul, so we don't think just with the brain anyway. During zazen the consciousness of the left hemisphere becomes less intense and the soul in the cells can receive transmissions from the cosmic consciousness. That is what I mean when I speak of body consciousness, bio-consciousness.

Nowadays the right hemisphere of the brain, the seat of intuition and instinct, has grown weak; but we can reconnect it through zazen.

When a fly senses danger, instinctively it flies away. That form of sensation is body consciousness, but in most people today it is weak and we can no longer understand or sense danger.

You talk a lot about samu in Zen. Does intellectual work count?

If you don't ever work with your hands you become too intellectual. Professors are too intelligent and can become a little bit crazy.

Wisdom is not just a matter of the forebrain. True wisdom arises from both thalamus and hypothalamus. When both are strong you have great wisdom. But if you spend all your time reading philosophy only your forebrain is working, while your old brain grows weak. The two are out of balance and you become tired and nervous and sometimes a little crazy. Your memory grows weaker and weaker, and even though the forebrain is developed by books it is tired. When you start to grow old you lose your memory.

But through the hypothalamus things are engraved in the brain. Their essence remains in the subconscious and during zazen it revives. Not sexual ideas, not pleasant thoughts: the things that have made a profound impression on the body, they are what revive during zazen.

For me, the sutras, my master's talks, all those important things have marked not my memory but my thalamus, through the subconscious.

Accumulating facts to pass exams, on the other hand, was very hard work for me, and now I've forgotten them all.

During zazen, when I talk, *the words penetrate to your thalamus and become seeds that will grow; in five, ten, twenty years they will become wisdom.* That is the highest psychology.

What is mushin*?

Mushin: nonthought. D. T. Suzuki wrote at length on mushin. It's "nonthought," "unconsciously," "mind without thought," no-thought. It is the essence of Zen. Supposing you do something or want something in your ordinary life: if you act consciously, you are not mushin. If the impulse is expressed as conscious thought, it is not Zen. That is why training in a practice that involves the muscles and whole body is so important. It's important for speaking too. Most people speak after the brain has given them the order to do so. But if you become mushin, hishiryo, you can speak unconsciously, without thought.

Take a mondo*: if you ask a professor a question he has to think before he answers. But the Zen monk answers without thinking, unconsciously. That's why a Zen mondo is important.

It's the same with actions. The brain thinks and you act afterward. That is not mushin. *Mushin is the body thinking.* If you understand that, you can understand Zen. Most Zen stories have to do with mushin. Wisdom and intellectual learning are not the same. In everyday life, in conversations, most people think first and then answer; but very intelligent people use wisdom and do not think. They speak and answer through intuition. Book-learning is different from true knowledge. In time, one ceases using the brain to answer questions.

Through zazen you can understand how one can speak unconsciously. Your superficial brain rests and your inner brain becomes active and receives energy. In a mondo my answers come from the inner brain; the activity begins there. My inner brain answers you unconsciously, mushin. That's why a zen mondo is different from an oral examination at the university. Speaking out of one's book-learning is not wisdom. From long practice of zazen you will acquire this unconsciously: wisdom, not book-learning.

When I give a talk, for example, I must prepare what I am going to say. Learning first . . . and a bit of wisdom. But the moment I stand up in the hall I begin to talk unconsciously and I don't always stick to what I have prepared. I look at the faces and see whether I need to change my talk. There is no more plan, my words come out of the unconscious, and that is why they impress people so strongly. That is *teisho.* *

Buddhist philosophy and Zen philosophy do not entail knowledge alone. That is true of the martial arts too.

How should I act? If I have to think about everything I ought to do I will not be able to act effectively at all. So mushin is necesary; it enables the body to react without thinking. That is why the practice of zazen is so useful in the martial arts. If you think too long your opponent will be quicker than you.

Sometimes you want to act in a certain way, but unconsciously some thought comes and you make a mistake!

That is not really unconscious. You aren't concentrated enough, that's all; you're thinking about something else. If you develop the habit of concentrating, everything becomes mushin. But training is necessary. Afterward, it comes of itself.

First you have to train, for painting, for any art, for any type of work. Then afterward you become mushin. You don't have to think, "I want to make something beautiful or good." Most great painters create their works unconsciously. That is the activity of true art. For actors it's the same thing. If they think, they don't move the audience. If they act unconsciously their acting becomes beautiful and the audience feels that they are living their character. *When people think, there is no activity,* and you don't feel any *ki,* * any force of energy, when you watch them. When you think, your action is neither strong nor beautiful. Pigeons don't think and they are very beautiful. People in our age think too much and the result is that nobody is impressed.

The actions of people who practice zazen are unconsciously precise and right, and their manners become very beautiful, natural.

When you talk about the normal condition do you mean something that used to belong to all mankind and then got lost, or do you mean something else?

It is hard to explain. As it relates to the body, the "normal condition" is easy to understand; but in relation to consciousness it's not so easy.

Psychology, philosophy, religions have all tried to explain it: *the mind or spirit of God, or the nature of Buddha, for example, are the normal condition.* There are as many different concepts as there are religions, and every age and period has been preoccupied by the question.

In zazen, the normal condition of consciousness is hishiryo: nonthinking.

When you think all the time you are not in a normal condition; it's your imagination, your personal desires, that are expressing themselves. You think more and more, you're afraid, you grow anxious. And if it goes on too long, complications arise and even madness.

If you stop thinking, you return to the normal condition of consciousness. But then you go to sleep . . . While you sleep, consciousness stops. Dreams bring the subconscious to the surface; but when you dream you are not in a phase of deep sleep.

In zazen you can return to a normal condition. You don't sleep but your muscular tonus is right, and your consciousness becomes similar to that of sleep.

It is not easy to stop thinking during zazen. The process is that of Master Dogen's hishiryo and, to some degree, Jaspers's *nicht denken;* that is the basis of the Zen philosophy of normal consciousness.

Fushiryo * means to not-think; hishiryo means to think without thoughts. If you deliberately try to stop your personal consciousness you're still thinking. But "without thinking" is something you can experience during zazen. Thoughts arise, the subconscious appears, but you don't need to stop it; being natural is best.

How can you use your personal consciousness to stop thinking? By concentrating on your posture. When the posture is good the muscular tonus is right, and the state of consciousness is closely connected to muscular tonus. If your muscles can return to their normal condition, so can your consciousness. We have to balance, harmonize the two. If the tonus is weak consciousness takes over, and your thumbs droop, your head sags, and you are sad, melancholy.

When muscle tone is right, the thoughts of the personal consciousness cease and the subconscious rises to the surface. Some people have too many things buried in their subconscious. They are the cause of the modern ailments of the autonomic nervous system, neuroses, hysteria, insanity.

During zazen that all comes out. And after zazen everybody has a good face. When you look at people who don't practice, you will surely see the difference, and if you continue practicing for a long time they will strike you as a little bit "muddy" because through zazen you will have become pure and returned to a normal condition.

What does Zen contribute to the mind?

Nothing. You must not want anything or have any desires at all. Practice without purpose, and the effects will come afterward, automatically.

It is written in the *Shodoka, "You must neither strive for truth nor seek to lose your illusions."*

If illusions manifest themselves during zazen one should neither repress them nor follow them up. It is very important to have no object in mind, to make no "use" of zazen. *Zazen is not a means to something.* If we have a goal, an object, our life will be troubled. We must follow the Way naturally; if we have no object our life will not die.

In the twelve years I have spent in Europe I have seen many

students coming to practice zazen for some purpose or other, and they have not persevered. Sometimes they are very sincere in their search but in the end they grow tired and give up.

You must not use the Buddha or Zen to obtain anything whatsoever.

My master was always insisting upon the idea of mushotoku, no-profit.

That is the essence of Zen and of Buddhism: obtain without trying to obtain.

We repeat that every day when we chant the *Hannya Shingyo.* That is the highest and most authentic philosophy.

It's as if you were painting and consciously wanted to create a masterpiece; when the work was finished, it would never be better than mediocre. But if you are truly concentrated and have no object in mind, you may be able to create something beautiful.

The highest dimension of spiritual life is mushotoku, without a goal, no-profit.

IMPERMANENCE HERE AND NOW

Can you explain here and now?

It is consciousness of time and space. What is happening here and now is what matters. Don't think about the past or the future, but concentrate on here and now. When you urinate, just urinate; when you sleep, just sleep; when you eat, practice zazen, walk, make love, exactly the same. Concentrate on the present act and nothing else. If you are not happy here and now, you never will be.

How long does now last—an hour, a minute?

Much less, much more. *Now is already over,* it doesn't really exist. When I say "Now is what matters," I mean practice zazen now, not this evening or later. And in the course of zazen also: this breath now, concentrate now.

But now as a unit of time does not exist. If you think about it, it's already gone, in the past. There is no such thing as a now, so what is most important is to concentrate on the point, and it is the connection of this point to all the other points that forms the duration of concentrating-here-and-now, just as in geometry an alignment of points forms a line.

> *There is a passage in the* Shobogenzo* *called* Uji.* *Can you talk about that?*

Uji is the philosophy of time. *U* = existence, *ji* = time.

Dogen wrote very profoundly on the subject of uji: all existences are time and time is all existences. Time cannot come back. We can come back to here but we can never come back to now. It's over.

If the points of our life form a broken line, then our life is complicated and founded on error. But if we concentrate on now the line will draw itself out, straight, harmonious, and beautiful.

Humans are always poring over the line of the past or the line of the future, and seldom concentrating on the point of "now."

Even during zazen some people are thinking, "Last year I did this and tomorrow I'll do that . . . " They are not concentrating on their posture and they're soon slumped over.

You must be concentrated now. That is true of your entire life. It's very simple and very profound.

> *"The world exists but it is not real." What do you think about that?*

I'm always talking about ku. Ku is existence without noumenon. It exists but it doesn't exist. There is no substance.

I exist, but what does that mean? Is this me, my head, my feet, my skin? No. My cells, body, skin are changing all the time. Every seven years all the cells in our body are completely renewed. *Where is me? It's the same for everything in the world,* and for the world itself; it has no noumenon, it is ku.

> *But what is real?*

This world exists. Reality or not-reality is a metaphysical question, existing is a physical question. It is hard to compare the two.

Sometimes religions make mistakes on this point and create confusion. In true Zen there is no commentary on metaphysical problems, nor is there in Buddhism, nor in the Buddha's sutras, nor in the philosophy of Nagarjuna. There is no way to decide about conditions before birth, after death . . . They cannot be determined by concepts or by science. It is absurd to try to conceive of life after death; that is the sort of thing that mostly bothers egotistical people who want to be immortal. They are the prey of their own imaginations and of egotistical religions, the kind that tell you that if you give huge presents you will surely go to heaven . . .

This question cannot be decided by metaphysics or by rational thought, and the only answers come from the imagination. Dogen talks about it in the *Genjokoan. The world is real or it isn't real, as you please.* You turn the knob on your television set and a reality appears on the screen. You turn the knob in the other direction and it no longer exists. It's the same as death.

When we die the world goes on existing, but our own cosmos disappears. Our karma continues, however. Our blood becomes earth and clouds, and in that sense we never end. Our body never ends and our spirit never ends. Body and spirit are one.

But there can be no confirmation of metaphysical issues. True religions do not attempt to resolve such questions and have nothing to say about them. Only egotistical people worry about eternal life.

Why are there phenomena in the cosmos?

Phenomena exist; rivers, mountains, stars are the phenomena of the cosmos. Originally the cosmos was chaos. Phenomena appeared and go on continually transforming themselves. That is the fundamental cosmic power. Ku becomes phenomena.

The Shin Jin Mei* *talks about impermanence. Are Buddha and the Way and the cosmic order impermanent too?*

Yes. *Everything is impermanent, even the cosmic order.* Everything changes. If you understand that you have satori.

Westerners are always trying to make categories with their individual consciousness and cannot accept contradictions.

If you look only at the aspect of permanence, everything is

permanent. If you look only at the aspect of impermanence, everything is impermanent. Both aspects are true. You must understand both sides and not choose just one.

The body is important; we are born and we die, like bubbles appearing and disappearing on the surface of the stream. But the essence, the stream, never changes.

Father and mother meet. The child is conceived and becomes energy. It grows up and gets married and owns a house and a car and so forth, and in the end it dies. It goes into its coffin. The elements composing its body return to the earth, even if it is cremated, and become energy again. There is no real change, only apparent change, change of form. There is permanence.

Both states are essential. This is not a question of sense, it is a question of wisdom.

But above all, do not create distinctions with your personal consciousness because if you do you will always be half-wrong.

Is there anything that is not illusion, phenomenon?

Ku and shiki, void and form, are the same thing. Phenomena themselves are truth.

During zazen you should not drive away thoughts but you should not contribute to them. If you concentrate on your posture you don't need to worry about having a conscious experience of satori, illumination.

It is true that during zazen many illusions manifest themselves. What are these illusions? What is good? What is bad? It is very hard to lay down a standard. "I have to be handsome, I have to be good, I must not think about bad things, about sex." But everything is phenomenon. So if you just concentrate on your posture it becomes like a mirror. The mirror reflects many things but the mirror itself is unchanged. Illusions themselves are truth. That is what it says in the *Hannya Shingyo:* ku becomes phenomena, phenomena become ku, there is no separation.

I can understand that, but even that is a relative idea, and I'm asking, relative to what?

Shiki is illusion. But the illusion itself is truth. It includes everything. During zazen it is not necessary to reject illusions. Even bad things pass by. It is pointless to make a distinction between illusion and satori. Illusion itself is satori.

You should not distinguish between good and bad. Sometimes demons become God and sometimes God becomes demons. Our face is the same. Sometimes the human being is God or Buddha, sometimes a demon. It isn't God or Buddha all the time.

During zazen you don't think, but illusions come along. And with habit, when one's legs stop hurting, one thinks even more. Beginners think less, they concentrate on their posture, their knees hurt or their back. Once zazen becomes a habit, however, thoughts return automatically. But you must not contribute to the thoughts, you must concentrate, and then you become a mirror again.

Is there no way of getting to ku, to emptiness or the void, through thought?

Ku is not consciousness of emptiness. Ku is existence without noumenon. I exist, the table exists, the carrot in the kitchen exists but it has no noumenon. You too exist but have no noumenon.

In the last analysis, what has noumenon? The source of all life.

What is the source of all life? Today there are two theories: mechanism and vitalism. Nobody has found a final answer. I personally favor activity, energy. That is the essence of ourselves, our own originality which differs in each of us, like our faces, characters, the color of our hair.

What is me? At the last, we have no noumenon. It's ku, empty. This is not me. Nothing is me. Our characteristics are the result of our karma, our heredity, our blood. All we are is aggregates of the karma of our ancestors, our environment. We are constantly changing. Our cells, our bodies are changing all the time. In the end, we have no noumenon.

Some people are disconcerted by this, yet it is the true meaning of ku.

If you understand that, you understand the ego. The ego or self exists but it is nothing more than karma and interdependence.

The essence of the table is wood. The essence of wood is the tree. A flower is very beautiful. What is its essence? You can dissect it but you cannot find its essence, any more than you can find a noumenon in our body. So in the end you say, "Maybe the essence is activity," and then you discover that activity is an interrelationship, you discover our interdependence with the cosmos; and then you may consider that God or Buddha is our essence.

Buddha said, "Our essence is ku." Christ said, "Our essence is God." That means the activity of the cosmos, the activity of all the cosmic systems. We find the same mechanisms everywhere: in the stars, our bodies, each one of our cells, macrocosm, microcosm. They are all built the same way. What we must do is realize this cosmic system: if we follow it we are free; if we go against it our lives become difficult.

When you look through a microscope you see that everything is built the same way: atoms, neutrons, and in the end nothing. No form, no noumenon, microcosm, macrocosm, all is the same, ku. That is satori.

What is mu*?

It's zazen. Mu means "nothing" or "not" or "non," but it is not a negative idea. Mu is not relative to the fact of existing; it's nothing. It is very difficult to explain.

What is mu? Nothing and everything. It is a great koan; some people spend three years, five years thinking about it. In Rinzai Zen the great masters think about it every morning and their disciples think about it during zazen and it goes on for years. Mu does not exist. Mu exists, but without noumenon. A great koan. If you continue zazen you can understand it.

SATORI

Can you talk about satori?

You can't understand it with your brain. If you practice zazen, on the other hand, you can experience satori unconsciously. The posture of zazen itself is satori.

Satori is the return to the normal, original condition. It is the consciousness of the newborn baby. Christ said the same thing, that we must return to the true original condition, without karma, without complications. Unlike what many people think, *satori is not some special state, but simply a return to the original condition.*

Through the practice of zazen one becomes peaceful. Through one's body one can discover the consciousness of satori. So posture is very important. You can't discover satori with your head in your hands like Rodin's thinker. That is why people in the East respect the posture of the Buddha. It is the highest posture of the human body.

Chimpanzees and babies cannot experience satori. Babies are in their original condition but then karma obscures it, and we must regain that condition. Chimpanzees don't need to; they are always in their original condition. Only human beings have lost it and become complicated and so they must regain it. The original condition is the spirit or mind of God, or Buddha-nature.

Is satori difficult to experience?

No, it is your normal state. Zazen helps you. You begin to practice, you practice again and again, and it becomes easy.

You say that satori is unconscious and one can't be aware of it. But can one be aware that one has not experienced it?

If you say, "I have satori," you are cuckoo. Nobody knows. I don't know either. Even at the moment of death you cannot know. If you think, "I have experienced satori," you are limiting satori by your conscious thought. *When you say, "That's it, now I've got satori," you are setting a limit, making a category,* and that is not true satori but a narrow satori.

Satori is boundless, it is cosmic consciousness, and we cannot "know" what it is. Total wisdom is true satori.

"Is it possible to understand that one has not experienced satori?" You don't need to worry about satori.

Buddha spoke of different states of meditation corresponding to different experiences. Is there something like that in Zen?

In Zen there are no degrees, no steps. If you practice zazen here and now you have true satori. Here and now, no degrees; that's very important.

When you're thirty years old you don't need to act like somebody who is eighty years old. At thirty you must be thirty, not like an old man.

Thoughts differ at different ages and satori differs too. The understanding of a man of thirty is not that of a man of eighty. No grades, here and now, no degrees.

You don't need to tell yourself, "I've got to become Buddha, I've got to experience satori." If you're twenty or thirty years old you must understand the satori of a young person. But satori, what is it? Simply truth, understanding the cosmic system, cosmic truth. And you cannot harmonize with the cosmic system until you have let go of everything.

But what are the degrees of satori? You said that Buddha had a great satori.

Never mind degrees. It's pointless to ask yourself during zazen, "What degree of satori have I reached?" One can't compare, or say that one is more profound or more infinite than another.

For example, in regard to the trivial matters of everyday life, zazen can make you see your mistakes. When you understand, and apply what you have understood, that is satori. It's little and at the same time great.

Understanding objectively is not the same as understanding subjectively. A small object can become the source of a great subjective satori. Master Kyogen was sweeping his garden one day and he experienced satori when a tile struck a piece of bamboo. The object itself is not important. There are millions of similar phenomena, but he had one satori.

Gensha was leaving his temple to go on a trip and stubbed his big toe on a stone. "Where does the pain come from?" he asked, and experienced satori. A lot of people stub their toes and don't get satori.

You cannot make degrees, either objective or subjective. Zen is the direct route that takes you to the summit, like an aerial cable car in the Alps.

What is kensho*?

Looking at one's own nature, seeing one's satori. It is a technical term used in Rinzai Zen. It is the master who certifies the satori. Kensho is the same as the "know thyself" of the ancients. We have no noumenon. If you understand that, it's satori. You return to the cosmic order.

That is the satori of Shakyamuni Buddha under the Bodhi tree. He understood that he had no noumenon, that he was connected to the cosmic order, the cosmic power, and then he experienced satori. When he stood up again he had solved everything. In forty-nine days his entire karma was liberated. Every day a girl brought milk for him to drink and gave him a massage. And in the end he understood that there was no noumenon. Nothing. The only noumenon is the fundamental cosmic power. Buddha's satori is that. It's the same during zazen, and if you believe you will not need kensho. During zazen you are connected to the cosmic order.

Have you experienced satori, Master Deshimaru?

I don't know!

You must not seek or desire satori. People who ask questions like that want to experience satori. Dogen lays great stress on this principle of Soto Zen: satori exists in us long before we are born. Ku is satori. Both ku and satori are without noumenon and what they mean is existence without noumenon. *Since satori is already in us, why should we try to get it?*

But if our life is full of passions and desires, if it is complicated, then we should practice zazen in order to return to our normal condition. Zazen itself is satori.

The way to return to a normal condition is through a good posture, correct breathing, silence.

To ask "Do you have satori?" shows that one has not understood true Zen.

The right answer is only "No, I do not have satori. I practice zazen because zazen itself is satori."

Here and now is what matters most.

Even if in the past one has imagined that one experienced satori, but here and now one is no longer in a normal condition, no longer practicing zazen, that other satori means nothing at all and it no longer exists.

Ceasing to practice zazen is ceasing satori. Satori cannot be a past experience; it is here and now.

Until death there can be no total satori; that happens in our coffin.

If I answer, "Yes, I have satori," that is not true satori.

If you ask somebody, "Are you good?" and the person answers "Yes, I am," it is pretty likely that the person is not so good as he or she claims to be; otherwise, the answer would have been more modest, "Not so very," or "I have no idea . . . "

Ask a madman if he's crazy, and he will tell you he isn't; on the contrary, he is absolutely in his right mind . . .

The same holds true for satori.

Most people live like satori's fools; they spend their lives in a tangle of passions, desires, illusions.

That is why Buddha or God exists, and what they mean is the one real truth of the universe, true satori, without illusions, without passions.

By practicing zazen you can return to a normal condition and approach God or Buddha.

To say that one has satori means in reality that one is in an abnormal condition, like the madman, like most people, for whom a normal condition means money, good food, honors, sex, clothes, cars, and so forth.

Yet all of those are only vain illusions of existence and they appear as such in the moment of death. When the body is put into its coffin, the body itself is an illusion.

When we understand this, our life gains new strength and we no longer need to be afraid of anything or delude ourselves with decoration.

Our life becomes peaceful and we have true inner freedom. That is the meaning of satori.

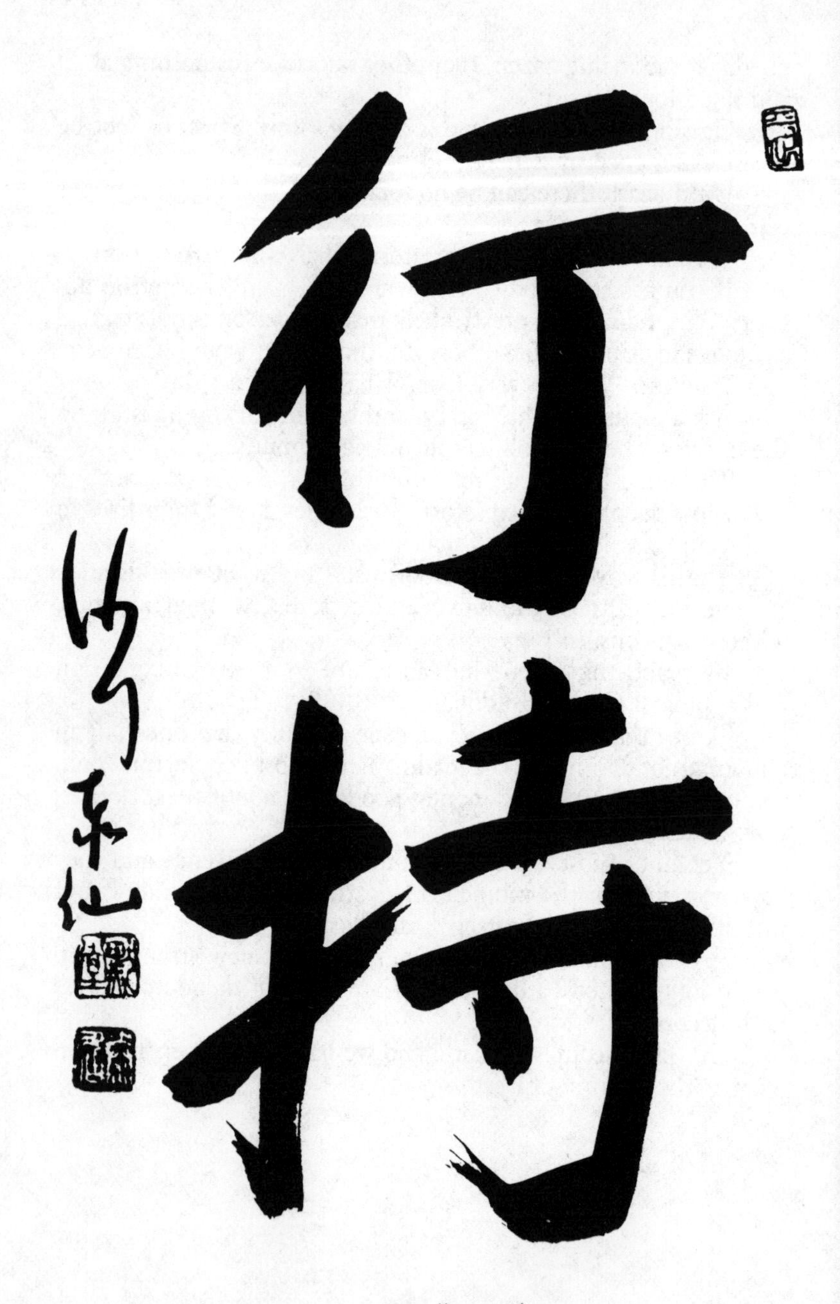

gyo ji, practice

PRACTICE

ZAZEN

You often say that everything is Zen; so why does one have to practice?

The only knowledge most people have of Zen is through books or the martial arts or ikebana (flower arranging) or chado (the tea ceremony). These things are all part of Zen, just as every phenomenon is part of Zen, even toilet paper is Zen. But if you don't have the experience of zazen you will understand nothing of Zen, because zazen contains the spirit of Zen. Without that the rest have nothing to do with Zen.

The essence of Buddhism is in the practice of zazen.

Many scholars lecture on Zen most learnedly and correctly, but they have no experience of zazen because they are professors and not monks. If you have a glass full of liquid you can discourse forever on its qualities, discuss whether it is cold, warm, whether it is really and truly composed of H_20, or mineral water, or saki. *Zazen is drinking it.*

One day a blind man wrapped his arms around an elephant's leg and concluded that he was holding a warm tree trunk. From the blind man's point of view that was not wrong, but neither was it the truth.

Scholars stand outside Reality and Essence; it is only once you have understood the essence of Zen that you can say everything is Zen.

You can have an intellectual understanding of what is meant by concentration, "here and now," the philosophy of time-space, no-profit and nondualism. *But the true essence is meditation, which consists of looking at oneself—on the inside.*

All I teach you is the method you can use to understand yourselves, to answer the question, what is the self?

Without the practice of zazen there is no Zen. If you practice zazen your whole life becomes Zen, toilet paper becomes Zen. But without zazen Zen is nothing! A beautiful temple where people do not practice is a temple for tourists, for ceremonies, a cemetery.

Without zazen meditation, books about Zen are worthless.

But if you practice zazen, with or without a temple, that is true Zen, even if you're not a monk, even if you're inside a prison. Zazen is right breathing, right state of mind, right posture. It is not stopping thoughts but letting them pass by, always coming back to the posture so that the posture will not give way.

If you concentrate on breathing and posture, the attitude of mind automatically comes right and wisdom is manifested unconsciously.

Is it possible to talk about progress in the practice of zazen?

If you practice every day, every day is progress. The mind is always changing.

If you practice zazen only once, that once is progress.

But the progress I mean has nothing to do with the steps of a stairway leading to satori at the top. If you practice zazen, here and now you can become like Buddha, like God. *There are no degrees.*

True Zen coincides with each person's here and now. If you are truly without any goal or desire for profit, truly mushotoku, then you realize Buddha, God. Mushotoku is extremely hard to practice in everyday life, but during zazen, when you are not trying to get anything, when you are not saying, "I must experience satori, I must become healthy, I must become Buddha, maybe I am now," then you can know what mushotoku is.

It is hard to let go of the ego, but if you practice zazen you can become mushotoku.

Why are Christ and Buddha and all the saints and sages great? Because they let go of the ego. Jesus and Shakyamuni were men but they abandoned their egos and became mushotoku, and then they became Christ and Buddha.

The zazen of young people is not the same as that of people forty, fifty, sixty years old. It's not a question of progress. When you're young you must live a young life.

It is the same with the posture of men and the posture of women: they are different. Every zazen is different. So you must find your own zazen. You must find your bad points. When I correct postures, I see some people leaning this way and some leaning that way; when I look at you from the back I see what is not balanced, even though you may feel very comfortable in your posture yourself. But you must correct yourself and eliminate the bad points. If you can find your right attitude, then you will have an original posture, a beautiful posture. Each one of us has to find his or her own originality and then each one of us becomes beautiful.

What is shikantaza? What is hishiryo?

Shikantaza? Only zazen; concentration on the act of zazen. Don't imagine that it means you must not go to the bathroom, or eat or sleep. That is not what shikantaza means; it means that *zazen conducts our life,* zazen is the center of our life. You must not get shikantaza mixed up with problems of consciousness.

During zazen you cannot stop thinking all the time; that is impossible. Sometimes you think, sometimes you observe. Only you do it unconsciously. You cannot prolong concentration indefinitely. You observe the buttocks of the woman in front of you, or you fantasize . . . It's hard to be concentrated all the time. Thoughts come. Let them go, do not concentrate on personal thoughts.

Hishiryo is the infinite thought of the brain, cosmic thought, not thoughts about little things but thought that includes the whole cosmos.

Would you advise a sick person to practice zazen as a form of treatment?

Getting well is an object. So I never tell anybody to practice zazen in order to get well. But if you believe in it and if you want to help, then you can advise someone to practice zazen. Sometimes

I say so, sometimes I don't; each person is different, and for each person the means and method must be different.

If I want fat people to practice I tell them, "Don't come, eat chocolate instead, zazen is difficult, very painful." Then they follow me. The traditional rule is that a person must be rejected three times before he is allowed in. He is told, "Zazen is difficult! There are too many people here already. Why do you want to practice zazen? You want satori? You're crazy. Go away."

Sometimes people ask me why I practice zazen and I never know what to say.

The answer is different for each person. The first time I asked my master Kodo Sawaki what the advantages of zazen were, he said, "Nothing." That answer aroused my interest at once. But one of my friends, hearing the same answer, got up and walked out. I was caught.

What is the best answer? For some people you must answer as though they were children: "If you practice zazen you will become strong . . . " But if Kodo Sawaki had answered me by talking about strength and good health I would have been less impressed and perhaps I would not have stayed with it. But that answer, "Nothing," made such an impression on me that I am still practicing zazen today.

In any event, the object of zazen is mushotoku, no-profit. But each person is different, and before you answer you must look the person in the face.

The merits of zazen are infinite.

Why is zazen more effective at sunset?

It is more effective to practice at sunset or at sunrise because the cells of our bodies change then. They change twice each day. In the evening we settle, our cells become less active. In the morning they become active again. So it is good to get up early in the morning. Nowadays many people do the opposite; they become active only after the sun has set, and when it rises they go to sleep.

It is very good to practice zazen at twilight and at dawn. It gives us energy, infuses activity into our cells. Those are the best times of day.

What do you think of yoga in comparison with zazen?

Zazen comes more easily to people who have already practiced yoga, but the spirit of yoga and the spirit of zazen are totally different. Yoga follows the traditional religion of India, based on asceticism and mortifications. Buddha turned away from that and concentrated solely on the posture that is now called zazen. That is why the people of the East respect not just the Buddha himself but his posture as well. Nobody bows down before a person standing on his head, but people do bow down before the zazen posture.

How does one practice zazen alone at home?

Practicing zazen alone is hard; the atmosphere in the dojo, the master's presence, and the presence of other disciples are a great help to meditation. My master often used to say that when he had to practice zazen alone, without his disciples, it was hard for him. There is emulation in the dojo; it keeps you from giving way the first moment you feel tired or have a twinge of pain. Fear of the kyosaku* and fear of disturbing those around you are stimulants. And the master, constantly correcting your posture, prevents you from getting into bad habits and growing sleepy. When we practice zazen together each zazen is as though it were the first.

But if for one reason or another you cannot come to the dojo, then choose a quiet place to practice zazen, far from noise and the telephone and your family (do not impose your meditation upon them). Sit for twenty to thirty minutes, concentrating on posture, breathing and attitude of mind. Be vigilant; nobody is there to correct you. Do not lose patience, do not drowse, and be especially careful to keep your chin in; learn how to face pain. It is important not to lose touch with my teaching, so come to the dojo now and then and your mistakes can be corrected. The inability to come must not become an obsession with you; the best thing to do is to concentrate on your work, on every moment of life. I always use the image of the drop of water that ultimately, by its regularity, can wear away the hardest stone. You must want to come even if you can't—that's what matters—but it must not become an obligation. This attitude will beget good karma.

Does our zazen have any effect outside ourselves?

Yes, your zazen influences the whole cosmos. It's the same if you make a fist and threaten someone. The statue of Christ, the statue of Buddha also have influence; they calm. You are living Christs and Buddhas, and the zazen posture is the highest posture. When my master was young he worked in the kitchen of a temple and practiced zazen every day in a corner of the garden or in a shed. One day a great monk who sometimes misused and berated him opened the door and saw him there. His posture was so beautiful that the other man quietly shut the door again and went away without a word. One old person who was always scolding him gave him some money once when he happened to see his posture. Why is the Buddha's posture respected in Asia? Because it is the highest. When we practice zazen, that alone is the substance of our specific nature, our originality.

Why do people respect me? Because I practice zazen. I am not so wonderfully intelligent or perfect, but my zazen posture influences everybody. My zazen posture is my noumenon.

POSTURE

Why do my knees hurt?

It's you who are hurting and not somebody else. You suffer with your head; you must understand the mind's share in pain. But it is also true that when you begin to practice zazen your body is not used to the posture; it is accustomed to all the comforts of modern life. But we need to go back to the original seated posture. After a while, it becomes natural and one no longer suffers beginner's pains.

Is it possible to eliminate pain during zazen?

Beginners suffer because they are not used to it and because their consciousness is not normal. Today you're in pain. Tomorrow you're not. The body changes; it is different every day. We are influenced by what we eat, by the environment, humidity, climate, heat . . . The morning is different from noontime and the evening is different again. We are influenced by other people too.

If you practice for too long a time you feel pain. Women are affected by menstruation; they are more sensitive then. Some people find it very difficult to practice after they have had sexual intercourse. Others not. Sexual intercourse during a sesshin is not good. The muscles become too soft; they relax too much. That is why yoga and the traditional religions in India laid such stress on asceticism.

Mahayana Buddhism does not attach importance to asceticism. *Too much denial does not lead to a normal condition.* Forcing oneself to refuse things is not good, especially as conditions differ in young people and older ones. Balance is always very important. If you stop having sexual intercourse but are thinking about sex all the time then that's not the best solution. When you force yourself too much, then the body moves during zazen. So sometimes you should have intercourse and your zazen will get better!

What we eat is important, too, during sesshins. It is best not to eat too much meat; it creates desires. It is better to avoid meat. But it is not wise to say, "You must eat no meat." Meat is necessary, especially for Westerners. But if you eat too much of it you may have many and intense sexual yearnings. That is why very little meat is served during sesshins. People react differently. When they are tired meat can be a medicine. Each person has to find his own rhythm and his own diet.

Never mind if you're in pain. You need to learn patience. The pain will go away. If you're in pain during zazen and you think about it, it gets worse. But if you ask for the kyosaku, sometimes it goes away. You can seldom feel pain in more than one place at the same time. As a rule there is only one painful point and the kyosaku relieves it.

During zazen, the kyosaku does not hurt. It restores balance. That is why it is given between the neck and shoulders. In Japanese massage it is not the sick or painful organ that is touched; the masseur touches a point on the meridian corresponding to that organ and the pain goes away.

"Chin in" is very important. If you draw in the chin and stretch the back of the neck, the pain goes away more easily.

And if it really hurts too much you can change legs.

What is the meaning of the position of the hands in zazen?

The left hand cradled in the right is the best position for concentration, for retaining energy. If you are drowsy your thumbs droop; if you are nervous they stick up. By observing them you can check and regulate, and take yourself "in hand" again. By looking at your fingers the master can understand your state of mind at once. The yogis meditate with their fingers in a circle. That is good, but the zazen position is better. Compare for yourself; you can judge which is better for concentration.

All the masters in China and Japan have studied this point. I myself questioned my own master about it, and finally decided that this was the best position.

I am always saying, "When you want to concentrate, put your mind in your left hand." Why the left hand? Because the right hand is tired, you're always using it.

Should you press hard with your thumbs or should they be just touching?

Just touching. Don't press hard. The hands must be perpendicular to the abdomen. They express the condition of your consciousness.

It is a very delicate thing. I do not need to look inside your brain. By your fingers I can understand your karma, your destiny. They are very revealing, and every day their shape changes during zazen.

By regulating your hands and the connection of your thumbs you can relax the tension in your shoulders, let them fall naturally.

Is it possible to close your eyes during zazen?

The position of the eyes in zazen is most important. Concentrating their gaze on one spot makes some people blink all the time. In fact, your gaze should reach the ground about a yard ahead of you and should not move or stare at the buttocks of the lady in front.

Some people shut their eyes, and then they begin to drowse.

In the past, dojos were very dark and the monks often slept because if you sit for a long time your brain becomes completely calm, you stop thinking, your mind goes from nonthinking to nonthinking and you fall asleep.

If you cannot manage to concentrate because you are too nervous or anxious, it is possible to shut your eyes for a little while, then open them again. Some people open them too wide and start staring at the sky, then fall into a sort of ecstasy or trance.

The true and correct position in zazen is to let the gaze fall a yard in front of you, keeping your eyes half-open.

Should the kyosakus correct people's postures?

Yes, if they know how. No, if they don't.

It is tricky to correct postures. You must have long experience.

I correct you and you must understand what I have changed: chin in, extend the pelvis or stretch the back of the neck or let the shoulders fall. I have been saying those same things over and over again for twelve years! The most important of all are the chin drawn in and the back of the neck stretched out. Push the sky with your head, push the ground with your knees. The position of hands and fingers is important too. The other points are more difficult to put right, and mistakes can have serious consequences. That is a job for the master, because of his experience, and the senior monks. But everybody understands "chin in." Some people are too tense. The forearms should not be stuck to the ribs.

But overcorrecting is not good either. When people are concentrated it is important not to disturb them by correcting. Wait until the next time. Sometimes I wait a month or more, because it's a delicate matter. The attitude is important. If the attitude is good it is not necessary to correct the posture. You must keep watch, and pick out the important point. If you correct something that doesn't need it or is not the main point, it won't do any good at all. You must correct exactly when the person can really understand where the posture is wrong.

Understanding is the essence of Zen. Too much teaching is not good. A very bad posture should be corrected, but only a very bad one. It is difficult with beginners and one has to be indulgent. Teaching too much at once is a mistake. You must do it little by little, gently; that way the teaching goes deep.

Can you talk about breathing during zazen?

I will try, but it is not easy. Traditionally, the masters never taught it. In yoga, on the other hand, it's the first thing you learn. But in zazen breathing is not taught. When your posture is right you automatically arrive at the right breathing. To show you properly, I would have to take off all my clothes, but you must understand through your own body.

A short, natural inhalation at the level of the solar plexus. Then, breathe out, pushing down on the intestines beneath the navel.

*Anapanasati** is breathing out, the Buddha's breathing. It was through anapanasati that he found satori under the Bodhi tree.

You don't need to breathe in, only out. Even after you have let out all your breath you can still breathe more tiny, tiny, tiny breaths.

When I chant the sutras my breath is very long because I am used to breathing out. As I breathe out there is a tiny in-and-out movement of air in the nostrils so I can go for a long time. But I have been training for forty years.

First you must understand with your brain, and then practice. This method of breathing can help you to live a long life. Most of the people in the Orient who live to be very old breathe this way; so I say you must concentrate on breathing out.

During *kin-hin,** if I moved at the rate of my own breathing everybody behind me would be standing still. So I breathe more often, to harmonize with you. One takes a step forward with each breath; so someone who breathes only once or twice a minute is covering very little ground.

In kin-hin you must push the floor with the big toe, the thumb inside the left fist. You can feel the energy all through the pelvic region. This breathing is used in the martial arts, which are not sports. The *hara,** the center of energy below the navel, has to be strong. To understand this kind of breathing, however, just chanting sutras is enough. Ceremonies and chanting sutras are perfect for training your breathing. When you chant, you must go all the way to the end of your breath. It's good training. Professor Herrigel talked about it in his book on archery. He studied that art for six years. At first he thought the master was crazy but at the end he abandoned all his book-learning and philosophy, and then he improved. He went to Japan to study true Zen. They told him, "It is very difficult. If you want to study Zen you should practice a martial art first." Herrigel was very good at shooting with a rifle so he took up archery. But he worked six years before he understood how to breathe. My master said, "If he had come to me first, it wouldn't have taken him nearly so long."

He succeeded when he understood "push down on the intestines," and not before. Judo also trains breathing, but most people don't know about it. Breathing doesn't come into it until the second or third dan or degree.

Herrigel understood unconsciously: the arrow is released at the end of the outward breath. It's the same in judo: breathing out you are strong, breathing in you are weak. You must overcome your adversary while he is breathing in. When a man is breathing in, I can kill him with one finger. You don't need a knife. I tried it on a man when I was young. I didn't really kill him, I only knocked him down. But at the end of the inward breath there is a weak moment. Breathing out, on the other hand, you can receive a blow and it doesn't affect you, you don't even move.

That is why yoga breathing is not at all effective for the martial arts. The Japanese do not care for yoga. Nobody practices it in Japan because people there know about Zen breathing. Breathing is very important for massages, too, and for fencing. And if you really understand, you can use that method of breathing in everyday life.

In a conversation, when you get excited about something, if you breathe as I have taught you it will calm you down again. The heart is massaged, the lungs fill. People who practice zazen become brave because of the downward thrust against the diaphragm. They take little things without a fuss and are less afraid.

One time—it was during the Russo-Japanese War—the soldiers in the trenches were so scared they were firing over their heads without even looking. Their captain was terrified too. My master poked his head out to see what was happening and—there was nobody there. He gave the captain a kick, grabbed a flag, and ran out to occupy the enemy position. The major wanted to know who was leading the men. "It's a Zen monk!" they told him. "I'm not surprised, they are brave and very efficient!"

Through the body, through breathing, one becomes calm

and wise, unconsciously. Ideas quit the body. If you practice zazen you will become used to it.

You think, "Maybe Sensei [Master] breathes like that from the beginning to the end of zazen." No. Sometimes I forget; but it is a habit with me in everyday life. Find your own way yourself. Concentrate on breathing out, like a cow when it moos.

If you spend more time breathing in you grow weak. Breathing in, you catch cold, you sniff. It's the same when you cry. But when you are happy, when you laugh, you breathe out. You can use your breathing to control your mind and attitude. It is important and not so difficult. But people forget. When you are sad or weak, concentrate on breathing out and your state of mind will change.

You can regulate your life and your emotions by your breathing.

Why is there so much emphasis on breathing out?

There is a balance, always, between taking in and giving out. But the conditions of modern civilization are destroying that balance: people are always wanting to take things in, to possess things, to possess power, to possess other people. Nobody thinks about being.

What is the right attitude of mind during zazen?

That is a most important point. The three main things in zazen are posture, breathing, and attitude of mind—and correctly practiced, they lead to the very principle of zazen: hishiryo consciousness, thinking without thinking. You cannot stop thinking entirely during zazen. In fact, you think even more than usual because there are also the thoughts that come from the past. In your ordinary activities you don't pay attention to them, but during zazen you can see the thoughts coming: "Maybe my wife is two-timing me." "Today I have a payment to make and I must remember to stop at the bank on my way out of the dojo." You cannot stop your thoughts.

Some forms of meditation teach that you must not think. Others say you must think about God. You must form images of

God or beautiful things, or you must think about a koan or some philosophical problem.

That is not the right attitude. You cannot go on without thinking for any length of time and if you try to concentrate on just one thing, such as "What is ku?" or "What is mu?" it is very difficult. It's the same as trying to stop thinking altogether.

In Zen what you must do is let your thoughts pass by. *As soon as a thought arises, let it go.* If money comes, or a young lady, or sex, or food or Buddha or God or Zen, let it go. In zazen, concentrate on your posture and let everything else go by. After a while, what is in the subconscious rises to the surface because when conscious thinking stops the subconscious mind can be expressed.

Freud and Jung wrote about it. Jung was a profound psychologist. He studied Zen, which he knew through the books of D. T. Suzuki. But he had no experience of zazen, and it is impossible to understand if one does not practice.

If you practice zazen you can understand the subconscious coming back to the surface. You must let it come up and in the end it wears itself out: one year ago, five years ago, when you were a baby. And you get back to what is original, to complete purity. That is satori. Not a special state, not a condition of transcendent consciousness.

During zazen you must let everything go by; but willing yourself not to think is also thinking. Let your thoughts go, do not follow them.

What kind of concentration is right for zazen?

It differs for every person. You must find your own way. Beginners need to concentrate consciously, to some extent; later, if they continue, they can concentrate unconsciously. And in the end, zazen becomes unconscious concentration. That is the ultimate state of zazen.

In the beginning you need to concentrate on posture, breathing, the fingers, and so forth. But if you concentrate on your fingers alone your mouth may drop open. And while you are concentrating on your fingers or on keeping your chin in, you must also be concentrating on every other point of the posture and on your breathing. It is hard to do all that at once, and *you are extremely busy during zazen.* But with habit, it happens unconsciously.

The posture influences your everyday life and you can acquire the ability to concentrate unconsciously on each thing. *When you concentrate unconsciously you don't grow tired.* When you concentrate deliberately you tire much more quickly.

In connection with concentration and observation: why is it necessary to observe?

I didn't say that you must tell yourself, "Now I have to observe my bad karma. I am obsessed with sex, Sensei told me so . . ." You don't need to be looking for things to observe; but if something comes unconsciously, for no reason, then you can. It will happen inevitably because it is not possible to remain concentrated all the time.

When you concentrate on your posture you forget everything, so it's not right to try to observe at that point. If you say, "I must stop thinking," you have set yourself a goal. "I have to concentrate" that's a goal too. It's better just to be natural. But it is not good to be always thinking about something. To bring books or notebooks, like a student did one day, is not good. I gave him the kyosaku. "But Sensei, it's easy to learn and remember things here and at home it's hard!" You must bring nothing into this dojo—I don't mean just notebooks—no problem from your brain. If you practice zazen you cut off everything. But thoughts are manifested through the subconscious.

What is the state of consciousness during zazen? It is the state of ultimate thought, hishiryo, thinking without thought. *Moving from nonthinking to thinking and from thinking to nonthinking.* Beyond thinking. It can't be explained. When you concentrate on posture, good breathing, your head exactly in the right place, everything is easier. Even so, thoughts arise—"Now I'm thinking"—and you begin to think objectively.

One can see one's own mind objectively.

You must be natural. It is only after zazen that there is a distinction between concentration and observation.

When your mind is too agitated to practice zazen can you count your breaths or concentrate on a syllable—mu, for example—in order to calm yourself down?

That is not the custom in Soto Zen. My master did not care for such practices. But some people use them during zazen. In Indian meditation you count breaths. Beginners can do it, but if you are counting that's all you concentrate on instead of the posture, so your posture is no good.

Shikantaza means concentrating only on posture, correcting posture, always coming back to posture. If I don't concentrate, after a very short time I begin to lose my posture. It is hard to concentrate on one's hands. But it's better to concentrate on the fingers than to count breaths.

Breathing is hard in itself, even for me and in spite of my forty years of practice.

I suppose I'm wrong, but I find that in the end I don't believe in posture alone. I believe in it as a means.

You do not understand Zen. *According to all the traditional treatises, in the end posture is the only thing that exists.* Zazen is the highest posture, the posture that has been transmitted since Buddha. When the posture is poor there is surely some illness. Everybody has a karma. Looking at your posture I can understand your karma and see what is wrong. If I explain to you but you don't follow my teaching, then the sickness comes out. That is why I say that mind and body can be healed by posture. It's very simple.

Western doctors treat people by acting on the body alone, while religious people take no interest in the body, only the spirit. That is why there is so much sickness nowadays. A real doctor sees what is wrong with one glance.

$$4 + 4 = 8$$
$$4 \times 4 = 16$$

The body to be healed, that's 4. Your mind also has to be taken care of, so that means a different specialist, or a priest, who looks after that. That's 4 + 4.

During zazen the body is cured; it experiences a great healing action. "Chin in" means that the balance of the autonomic nervous system is restored. There is also a great effect on the consciousness, the mind, and the result is 4 × 4 because it all takes place at the same time. That is the essence of Zen. The posture is the essence, the philosophy of Zen.

With its two wings an airplane can travel 500 miles in one hour. Could it travel 250 miles in one hour with only one wing? That's not possible. It's the same with body and mind.

Modern psychologists also talk about the influence of the fingers on the mind.

People think they can put their minds right through an act of will, and then they ask doctors to put their bodies right. Both must be done at one time.

When a priest or pastor wants to heal somebody's mind, he must also act upon the body.

The posture is not 4 + 4, it's 4 × 4. Very important.

But I find that I can't really believe that posture is the only thing that matters, that it is an end in itself.

Then what do you believe? When the posture is wrong, the person is not right. The body is very important. Body and mind are like the front and back of one sheet of paper.

I understand what you are trying to say. But what is the source of the sound of clapping hands? Where does it come from? *Body and mind are the same thing.* People in the West are always differentiating between body and mind. They're like a sheet of paper: you cannot buy the front of it without buying the back too. It's the same with the body.

Descartes was a dualist. Most people think, "My body is dead and my soul goes to heaven." That is why you are always thinking contradictions. That is what makes you sick. Body and mind are unity. Body is mind and mind is body. Modern physics has confirmed that. When a doctor operates, can he find the soul or spirit? Inside the skull, perhaps? But everything in the body is spirit or mind. Everything is spirit.

If you want to experience satori your body must be in good health, and the posture of zazen creates the best attitude of mind. That is why Orientals venerate the image of Buddha. Not the statue, but the posture. The posture in itself is satori.

If a person's head is always stuck out in front of him, the

person is not entirely in his right mind. It's like in yoga: nobody venerates the posture of a person standing on his head. Nobody respects an ugly posture, a face with the mouth gaping open. Only the true posture is respected. If you practice zazen people will certainly be impressed and respect you for it. The posture is like clapping hands. Where does the sound come from? Which hand? The sound and the hands are one thing. No separation. There are lots of koans about this point. The body and mind are like the two wings of a bird.

TRADITION

What place does tradition have in Zen?

Zen has always respected and protected tradition.

From the time of Buddha, it has always followed the tradition and never turned aside from it.

But on the other hand, Zen is always creating, adapting itself to every place and time. It is always fresh, as a spring leaping out of the ground.

What is the tradition? Very hard to explain, because what has been transmitted is the nature of Buddha, the essence of the spirit, beyond words, and it has been transmitted for centuries, *I shin den shin,** from my soul to your soul, from master to disciple.

From India to China, from China to Japan, and from Japan to Europe and America, Zen has changed place several times. To grow it needs fresh soil, it flees formalism and ritual paralysis.

Westerners often ask me if they will be capable of really understanding Zen. And I always answer that they will succeed far better than people in the East because they are fresh and new. "Only an empty bottle can be filled."

Sometimes, to educate their disciples, Zen masters have burned statues of the Buddha. In this dojo there is a very beautiful statue of the Buddha and I always bow down respectfully in front of it. Why? Because it is Buddha? Or because it cost a lot? In fact, it is to you I am bowing, because when you practice zazen you are living Buddhas.

You must not get this wrong: *Zen is beyond all religions.* Buddha is just a name. Only zazen is important; during zazen you are Buddha.

Why the ritual?

Sometimes it is necessary. *We are not animals.* One can teach through manners, gestures, ritual. Performing a ritual influences the attitude of mind of the persons performing it.

The form of the ritual does not have great importance. But through that ritual I can educate your mind inside yourself. I do not know European ritual but I have a profound knowledge of Zen ritual, so I use that. I am a Zen monk and I cannot teach Christian ritual. But the form is not so important.

There is no doubt that a very profound Christian monk can educate through ritual too. Great monks always teach through ritual, they influence their students' consciousness. At school a good teacher must always be watching the way his pupils behave. Nowadays teachers are not so good; all they teach is knowledge. Great teachers look at children's manners, their actions. By working on them children can be taught to act more exactly.

Why do we have to walk along the walls of the dojo and turn at right angles in the corners?

If you don't turn at the corner you'll walk into the wall and fall down.

The way you act is very important; it influences your consciousness. Crazy people do not behave precisely. They are like walking ghosts. When your consciousness is right you can walk straight and turn a right angle.

In the dojo you train yourself to be exact. When you enter the dojo you make a little pause, and you step in on the left side of the door with the left foot first. If you repeat that again and again it will influence your consciousness and you will learn to be precise habitually in your everyday life.

Why perform ceremonies?

A little bit of ceremony is necessary.

Every day?

Yes, every day. By repeating this ceremony every day your manners become beautiful. It is very good for your concentration. During the *Hannya Shingyo* you concentrate on breathing out, as during zazen, but in fact it's easier than during zazen. When you chant your breathing comes naturally, automatically, and unconsciously. By performing sampai, the prostration, you learn to be humble. Repeating the same gestures, the same things, is a very important part of education. Your karma changes. Your face changes, your manners change, your mind changes. The ceremony is simple. It is better to practice it than to watch it. It is not entertainment.

What is the meaning of the altar with the Buddha?

Those are decorations. *It is necessary to mark the center,* a sacred, holy center. And then there has to be a place for the kyosakus and the incense bowl and box, so that the altar can give off a delicate perfume all around. And then it's convenient for ceremonies.

Your explanation is amusing, but is it complete?

In a real temple there is a Buddha hall, a lecture hall, a ceremony hall, and also a dojo where you practice zazen. In that kind of dojo the altar is not large and the statue on it represents Manjusri* sitting on a lion. That is the rule. But a statue of Buddha is good, too; it doesn't matter. What matters is that the dojo have a center and a right and a left. If there's nothing, it is not practical.

Of course, there are lots of other meanings. The altar makes the atmosphere more pure, too, holier and more sacred. We can feel that. It is better than having nothing there at all. But in the end, there is no especially deep meaning about it, except, and most important, that it marks the center.

What is the meaning of gassho [the salutation with hands placed palm to palm]?

Gassho is the religious spirit.

In traditional religions you bow down before God and create a separation between God and yourself. In Zen, too, when you perform gassho you are recognizing God; and yet originally the Buddha did not agree with the traditional belief that there was God on one side and humans on the other, God good and humans bad.

When Buddha first came into the world he said, "I am the highest existence." (I don't believe he really said that because babies don't talk, but that is the legend handed down in the sutras.) From the moment of his birth he rejected all systems. "I am the highest existence"—that is, the highest human. Not a god, a human being.

At the time he was very revolutionary. And that is one reason why some Christians say Buddhism is a form of atheism or pantheism. And yet on some occasions, Buddha himself recognized God as the highest existence.

In truth, the human becomes God. That is why I say that when practicing zazen you become Buddha, God, or Christ. The same with gassho: *God and the left hand, self and the right hand.* When you join them in gassho you create complete unity.

There is respect, but without differentiation. You must not forget yourself. On the surface it seems very contradictory. Zen says you must abandon the self, but through gassho it is yourself that you harmonize with the cosmic system, with God. That is the meaning of gassho.

The brain is influenced by the hands. If you make a fist you are aggressive and the mind feels it. The shape taken by the hands influences the brain. Holding your arms level for gassho is not the same thing as hunching your back over or letting your shoulders droop.

How should your hands be in your everyday life? That is also important. The mind, attitude, changes depending on whether your arms are crossed in front of you or your hands are shoved in your pockets. If I put my hands behind my back and start walking, it's Napoleon. The hand position influences consciousness; psychology has explained it. It's a deep question.

How important are the sutras? Were they written by Buddha or by his disciples? Do they have authority or not?

When you look at a painted apple do you know whether it tastes good or not? Some people say you can't eat it. *It is not a real apple but it is a real answer.*

Great question, great problem. Buddhism and Buddha are badly misunderstood by our contemporaries. Buddha's disciples wrote things that were true and things that were false. The moment one hears, the moment one writes, one creates categories. Afterward, the words have to be put in the proper form. You have to correct things, otherwise people would not buy your books. You make changes. When I speak I am limited; I cannot express the whole of my thought. I think, and I want to say this or that but finding words is very difficult.

The sutras are not wrong but they do not carry the whole truth. The *Lotus Sutra,* the *Diamond Sutra**—those are right; but if you read the *Lotus Sutra* it will seem very strange to you. It is a novel, literature, like the painting of a real apple. *The painted apple is a real apple but you cannot eat it.* It's the same.

You must not read everything in the sutras. You must understand the true meaning beyond sutras. There are eight thousand volumes of the *Lotus Sutra,* six hundred of the *Hannya Shingyo;* all the sutras together total more than 80,000 volumes. If you wanted to study Buddhism through the sutras you would have to begin by reading 80,000 books. If you read only ten or a hundred you would know only a tiny portion of them. So what must you do?

Zen means going directly back to the mind of Buddha, who experienced satori under the Bodhi tree. You must have the same experience, with the same posture, the same breathing, the same state of mind. It is not necessary to read books: rather, have the experience here and now. If you read sutras all you will have is learning. You will become complicated and a little crazy. You will want to be arguing and discussing and you will not understand the essence of them.

Can the sutras be recited in another language, or does Japanese have some special important sounds that are a reason for not changing them?

In reality, the *Hannya Shingyo* is not Japanese or even Chinese; it has Sanskrit resonances, combined with Chinese and Japanese.

Predominantly, however, it is the old Chinese pronunciation mixed with Japanese pronunciation. Even the Japanese did not change it. It has been translated into modern Japanese, with beautiful phrases, but the modern translation is not used. You must penetrate its breath, rhythm, and original sound before you can create by yourself. The *Hannya Shingyo* is like the song of spring. Chanted at the end of zazen, it is also a breathing exercise, deep out-breathing. The pulsation of a unified vibration, together, all together.

Does that mean the sound is important?

Yes. That is why the same text has gone on being transmitted. In temples the monks do not use the version that is easy to understand. They use this mixture, in which some of the words have been changed to the Japanese pronunciation. It is neither Indian nor Chinese nor Japanese. The ideograms, though, the *kanjis*,* are Chinese and Japanese; *gya tei gya tei,* * the last words, are sinicized Sanskrit.

Modern Chinese no longer know how to read the old characters but most Japanese monks do. My French disciples understand and have good memories. That is why the Japanese who come here are surprised, and a Chinese person would be even more surprised.

The sutras are always talking about previous Buddhas. Who were they?

You must not make categories, or try to create mysteries. Shakyamuni Buddha understood through his body that the fundamental cosmic power existed and that he was one with that current. He forgot everything that had to do with himself; his body and his mind were in harmony and had become one with the cosmic power. He experienced it. You must have the experience yourself.

In the Shobogenzo *it says that a human is only a child of Buddha if he or she has been ordained.*

Yes, Master Dogen wrote that. What is your question?

What does it mean to be ordained?

It means to become Buddha's child! If you want to become Buddha's child, ask to be ordained. It is a formality, and not so important. If you want to be Christ's child, you should be baptized.

At first it's not necessary to become Buddha's child. But if you want to come closer, if you want to study and understand Buddha's mind then you must practice zazen, and if you are ordained you will be able to understand the tradition of Buddhism more deeply. If you cut off your hair and put on a black robe your state of mind will change. *Practice zazen once in a black kimono and once in your business suit, and you will feel the difference.* If you put on the kesa your spirit will change and you will not practice the same way. When the form changes the mind is not the same. When I was young I did not want to shave my head. My family and friends were against it. In the end I did it and I understood more deeply.

Why practice zazen, why become Buddha's child? It's the same question. Some people say, "You don't need to practice zazen, just read books and you can understand." If you limit yourself to written experience you can understand Buddhism with your intellect, but if you do not practice zazen you cannot come close to the Buddha-mind or understand the experience of Buddha.

What vows does one make when one becomes a monk?

The vow to practice zazen . . .

The rules, the precepts change from one century to another; a hundred, two hundred, a thousand, two thousand years, today, next year: everything changes. Of course, we must not kill or steal or lie; there are the same five or ten commandments in every religion.

But for the rest—sex, tobacco, alcohol—the rules change with the age. In Buddha's day there was no such thing as tobacco, so the sutras have nothing to say about it. All that has changed now, sexual customs as well. The precepts of Christian monks are quite different from those of Buddhist monks.

What counts is to have faith and practice zazen. If you

practice, your morals will improve. Your personality will be purified. You will become calm, not so bad-tempered as before, not so emotional. And so you change your karma.

Is it possible to change one's karma?

You can change your bad karma if you practice zazen. *It wears out and comes to an end.* Your life is transformed. During the ordination ceremony I read a long poem that has been translated into French and English—the ordination sutra. If you decide to become a monk the ordination itself makes a change. Your whole family will become happier. You become completely alone, you cut your bonds with your whole environment. Your inner spirit gains true freedom. Everything changes, the mind changes, the body changes. In your mind, you cut yourself free from all complications, and then you can follow the cosmic order. I had the experience myself.

When I was ordained by my master, Kodo Sawaki, everything changed. I had reached the last station, the terminus! No more worries about anything, no more need for money, no more bother over the family. Our affection becomes freer, stronger. I shaved my head and my family was not so pleased. My daughter cried, "Why has Daddy cut off his hair? Why has he run away to a temple?" But afterwards my family understood and became happy again.

It's karma that changes.

It may seem like a formality but it is very important: you put on the kesa, you practice zazen, and in the end you shave your head. The kesa is not just a piece of cloth. You must believe in it. If you look at it the way a dog would look at it, then there is no effect. Its meaning is very profound.

If you shave your head and put on the kesa and practice zazen you become truly free. My life was very complicated before, and that of my master Kodo Sawaki was even more complicated. He was poor and had a strong personality. I had the same characteristics. Sometimes I have a very strong ego; it's better that way for a Zen monk, because then it becomes possible to abandon it, to abandon everything.

My master always used to say, "*The fruit of the kaki is bitter but if you let it sit long enough it turns sweet.*" The bitter ego becomes the cosmic ego. The stronger the ego the better it gets, if you continue practicing zazen, and the cosmic ego you obtain at the end will be even stronger.

The worst people can become monks. Why is that?

When the master permits, worst can become best. That is Mahayana Buddhism. The worst passions, the worst *bonno** become the source of satori. When ice melts it produces a lot of water. Great bonno, great passions are transformed into great satori. A great master must transform them and shows his dimension by doing so.

Don't you think it is harder to be a Zen monk today in a big city than it was two thousand years ago in a Zen monastery?

Harder, easier, it depends on the person. People come to practice zazen here for one hour and afterward go out to live their lives . . . If you went to a monastery all you would think about would be getting out of it. "I want to go to the restaurant, I want to go see a woman, or my friends, etc."

People always have doubts in their heads. Which is harder?

The monks who live at Soji-ji or Eihei-ji are always wanting to make love at night, and they stay there only three months. But for an older person, retiring to a monastery, escaping from the world, is not so difficult. When a young man enters a monastery he soon wants to leave again; that's all he thinks about. Even at a sesshin lasting only a few days, like the one we had at Lodève, some people were forever counting how much time was left until the end.

What is easier is to practice zazen for an hour in the morning, or even twice a day, and be free the rest of the time. That's better! For the Japanese monks zazen is a business, a profession. But you, now, you want to practice zazen, so zazen is always fresh for you, it is not a business. When zazen becomes a business the true religious spirit dies.

Some people run away as soon as they cut off their hair. Up to the very minute of ordination they say, "I want to be a monk." Then they start thinking and they go away. Half of the people who become monks stop practicing zazen as soon as they're ordained. But life in a temple is very hard. You are always, always alone. And when you cut yourself off from society you become egotistical: you want to be calm all the time and practice zazen alone in the mountains! That's fine during sesshins, but it is hardly possible to go on that way forever. People give up. So I say that zazen must be like the drop of rain.

Otherwise, as soon as a person has become a monk he doesn't want to be one anymore. To be a bodhisattva is not the same as being a monk; it means wanting to become one. Being a monk means reaching the last station, the terminus. But it is better to make the trip than to arrive.

How far does the commitment of a bodhisattva go? In everyday life we make a lot of commitments that conflict with each other and take away all our freedom. Can the bodhisattva commitment liberate us?

That question comes up very often. When you get married, it's the same thing. *Sometimes it is necessary for a person to have a law, a limit, an ethic.* We are not the same as animals.

In Buddhism and Zen ordination is not a commitment. When you have been ordained, and if you continue to practice, even if you want to make mistakes you cannot. When you receive ordination your karma is transformed; even if you want to do something wrong you can't work up any enthusiasm about it. That happens automatically and naturally.

It is not a deliberate undertaking. I don't think it is the same in Christianity; but it is my belief that a *true religious ordination does not entail prohibitions.*

You automatically become unable to do wrong, and even if you continue doing wrong for a time the desire quickly dwindles. Through the body's actions the passions diminish unconsciously. There is no need to think one way or another way. True freedom! You can follow the cosmic order unconsciously, naturally, automatically.

During the ordination ceremony I never say, "You must do this, you must not do that . . . " *I give the ordination and you receive it;* your karma changes automatically. Zen ordination is not a legal undertaking. Of course you should not kill or steal or misbehave sexually or lie. Not lying is very hard. Not killing a mosquito is hard too. And you should not admire yourself or criticize others . . .

In Buddhism there are ten precepts, but they are not prohibitions. Buddha said, "If you practice zazen that is the greatest precept, and everything else vanishes." If you practice zazen your karma changes, everything gets better. The people who are drawn toward evil go away. The people who continue to practice become very good. If they make mistakes they become aware of them, or else they go away and stop practicing.

Can you explain the role of the bodhisattva in modern life?

There are no limits. If I were to explain, you would be tempted to limit the role of the bodhisattva to what I had said. Every day you must find out the duties of a bodhisattva.

They are not the kind of duties that come from a religious commandment. What you have to do is leap into the river to help those who are drowning, leap into the dangerous places. That is the bodhisattva's vocation.

Leap into difficulties, not run away from them. It's very hard. That is what the bodhisattva does to help others. First give food and water to others, only afterward to yourself.

"Please, you experience satori," says the bodhisattva. "I am going to help you to have that experience at any price, and afterward I shall try to have it myself."

Why does one never hear about women Buddhas?

Yes, yes, they exist. Many women have become disciples of Buddha, and quite often a master has been taught by an older woman. In the Asia of old, however, it was customary not to record a woman's name even if she was a source of wisdom and taught a master. Nowadays all that has changed; men and women are on an equal footing and a woman can perfectly well become a master.

*Kannon** is often represented as a woman; but in fact Kannon is beyond gender. Neither man nor woman: that is Mahayana Buddhism. Buddha's teaching is for men and women alike, and is beyond both. The distinction between masculine and feminine is a great problem for me in the French language. In Japanese the distinction does not exist for nouns the way it does in French; why *la* Seine and *le* Rhône? Why not *le* Seine and *la* Rhône? I find it very funny, comical. Maybe because the course of the Seine is softer, more feminine than that of the Rhône? *Buddha is beyond he-Buddha or she-Buddha!*

Oriental languages do not make that kind of category. The East did not create science, but it also did not set limits on religion. The same sentence, infinite in Chinese or Japanese, becomes full of categories in a Western language. Philosophy is very highly developed in the West, but it is all categories. Nietzsche came to a dead end; he said that people must embrace contradictions but he himself got tangled up in them and died insane . . .

What is the meaning of the kesa?

Dogen wrote two long texts on the subject of the kesa.

Zazen is the spiritual essence of Zen, and the kesa is its material essence. In Christianity, in Buddhism, people respect the Cross or statues and images of Buddha. In Zen, it's the kesa. People want objects of faith. There has to be something visible. What is the best material? Buddha thought about it and so have the masters. Clothes are often important. How to dress? That's why there are fashions, like the Parisian fashions that travel all over the world.

So in Zen, too, clothes are important: the white robe we wear is Japanese, the black robe is Chinese; the kesa is Indian. It is very important. It is the symbol of Buddha, like statues. But I like the kesa better than statues.

What is the symbol of the spiritual life? A disciple asked the Buddha that question and so the kesa was created. The seams represent rice paddies. You must use the most ordinary cloth. To make the first kesas people gathered winding-sheets or shrouds, the cloths used for women in childbirth, menstrual napkins, whatever had been soiled and nobody wanted anymore and was going to be thrown out. The pieces were washed and disinfected with ashes, assembled and sewn together, and became the monk's clothing, the highest clothing. The basest material became the purest garment, because everybody respects the monk's robe and kesa.

The basest material becomes the most pure: that is the whole foundation of Mahayana.

It's the same thing with our mind, our bonno. You don't need to look on the outside, only inside. If you look at yourself you will see that you're not so wonderful. Everybody is full of contradictions.

In the *Hokyo Zanmai* it says, "A rat in a hole and a tethered horse may be standing quietly, but inside they are longing to escape." It's the same with our minds during zazen. They're always looking for something. It's the same for me, and even for great masters. Buddha, too, suffered from this problem. It is the weakness of mankind.

Through zazen you can direct and regulate your mind. If the rat is weak it quickly dies. It's like the story of the taming of the shrew. If the mind is well-guided it can be changed. A weak person cannot become great. It is better to be strong and have strong illusions. If we have great illusions we will have a great satori.

The basest cloths become the symbol of the highest spirituality. That is the principle of Mahayana.

There are enormous contradictions in the human race. The forebrain and thalamus have conflicting functions. If we have a purely intellectual approach to life we are assailed by contradictions and are always suffering.

The kesa is very important; wearing it helps us and changes our karma, just like zazen. It is a symbol, and I believe in it. It is the symbol of my master. So I wear this kesa and am unafraid. For me it is the transmission of my master.

What is lowest becomes most high. Our worst mind becomes best, highest, most noble.

Why do great masters like Dogen or Nagarjuna, masters who practice mushotoku, treat the kesa as an object of veneration when they grow old, and study and write books about it?

The kesa is the essence of Buddhism, the symbol of the Buddha. Buddha gave a talk, attended by all his disciples, and at the end he picked a flower and turned it in his hand, and nobody understood except Mahakasyapa, who smiled. It was to him that Buddha transmitted his kesa, because Mahakasyapa had understood his spirit. He transmitted his kesa to him as the symbol of the true satori. Visible and material symbols of the Dharma are necessary. *Shiki soku ze ku, ku soku ze shiki**: emptiness becomes form and vice versa. The kesa is the highest material symbol.

Nowadays monks in Japan don't shave their heads anymore and hardly ever wear their kolomo. They bring it along for ceremonies in a suitcase, like actors. But the *rakusu** or kesa remains the symbol that divides profane from sacred. It is the symbol of the *sangha,** the community of people who practice zazen.

If I die it is not necessary to respect my person but it is necessary to respect my kesa, which is my true spirit, my satori, the *Dharma** itself. Studying the kesa is a great koan, the fundamental essence of the transmitted teaching, even if its shape and color have changed in the course of time.

What is the importance of the master in Zen? Can a disciple lead a dojo?

If there is no master, the disciple is like a blind man walking without anything to guide him. Dogen wrote about the absolute necessity for a master. If you practiced zazen without a master you would make mistakes. If you make mistakes your mind will go off the rails, a little bit or a lot. For beginners it is very difficult, and then they don't understand. I have taught you what consciousness is in the Zen of Master Dogen. I have explained from the very start what it means. If you follow a master your consciousness becomes more and more profound. The disciples who have been following me for a long time understand, by listening to me, and they are becoming more profound. Disciples may open a dojo if I give them permission. They represent the master.

How important is the dojo? Is it just to come see the master?

Why the master? I can practice zazen alone, myself.

There is only one master and many students. You and me and everybody. The master is alone and he has many disciples. I need every one of you. Do not pay attention to the others. Only you and me. But I have to see everybody and you have only to look at me. It is hard to practice zazen alone in your home because I cannot go visit you there. I understand your question.

Atmosphere is very important. There is an interdependence among all the people who practice, a reciprocal influence. If you are alone and I am alone here, the atmosphere would not be the same. *If there is only one log in the fireplace the fire will not be strong.* If there are a lot of logs the fire catches quickly. Today there was a very strong atmosphere, lots of logs blazing away. A wonderful fire. That is why the dojo is important. You can feel intense activity in it, but you feel it unconsciously. You don't need to think, "I am influencing other people," "I am being influenced by other people." It happens unconsciously.

If you don't want to practice zazen, I don't care. If you do want to practice, then you follow the cosmic life and I follow you. If nobody came (maybe a few people would continue at home), I myself could not practice zazen; it would be hard for me. I have been practicing for forty years now. I have tried to practice alone. I did it for a month or two. I am very sincere, and I like zazen very much; but it was extremely hard. Sometimes in my room, when I have been writing, I practice zazen unconsciously in front of my desk. If you go to the dojo unconsciously you follow the cosmic order.

When a person wants to practice zazen, does he or she always need a master?

Yes; at first it is necessary. A proper master. If you follow a blind man he doesn't lead anywhere and in the end you fall into the ditch. Without a master you cannot follow the Way. If you want the true Way a master is necessary. I show my disciples the direction to the Way, which is hard to see. If they don't look at me they go in the wrong direction. Without a master you cannot maintain a correct posture, breathing, and state of mind for very long. In zazen, you get up and quit as soon as you feel a little discomfort: "Today is a bad day, tomorrow maybe . . . "

With a master you must follow, and you can. Even if you don't want to perform samu you follow, thanks to the interdependence between master-friends-brothers-and-sisters of the holy sangha. Alone it's hard. Even Mahakasyapa followed Buddha, needed him. If you want to understand the true Way, the true Zen, a true master is necessary.

Nowadays people seem to be so weak; can a Zen master find strong, true disciples?

It's very easy, yes, because people are very intelligent. Of course, times have changed and conditions in big cities like Paris aren't the same as in the countryside. Educations differ, are specific to each place and period. Disciples are always changing.

You are here and you are surely sincere, honest, and good. I believe it. So the kyosaku is not necessary; I don't like to use it. Teaching by the kyosaku is not the best way. In ancient China masters taught solely with the stick. They never used words. Master Umon's school was called the "kyosaku school" because he never opened his mouth and used nothing but the stick to teach with his whole life long (he himself was nicknamed "Master Stick"). It was a powerful school in which the disciples became extremely strong. Questions were very profound and carefully chosen, and when you asked the master a question you would receive the kyosaku. One blow for every mistake.

Zen is spreading. Many people, some of them fervent Christians, are trying to practice it. How can this demand be met without changing the nature of Zen? You are the only one at your level and you can't be everywhere. Who can be qualified to help?

My disciples help; they follow my teaching.

True disciples always follow their teacher and do not deviate. Time helps, too; time will bring solutions.

Errors are eliminated. Truth is eternal.

Fifty or so of my disciples have understood what real Zen is, and, especially in my dojo, about ten have an absolutely exact knowledge of my teaching of zazen; they can represent me and continue my teaching. Their numbers are growing all the time, and so my teaching of the practice of Zen can be transmitted without too much difficulty. New groups can be formed without any danger that the right spirit will be lost, or the absolute rigor of the posture.

How can I know if I understand Zen?

It is the master who must certify the authenticity of your understanding; if you certify yourself, there is no true understanding.

Subjective certification of yourself and objective understanding by the master are both necessary. You say to yourself, "I understand, I understand . . ." People always want to create their own categories and sometimes they make mistakes. That is why words are needed.

In Rinzai Zen the teaching is very severe. In Soto it's not so difficult. You understand or you don't understand. For twenty years I myself kept asking my master questions, and he kept saying,, "Just practice zazen . . . shikantaza."

In Rinzai Zen there are words, koans, discussions about koans, and the master certifies. In Soto Zen, there is less of that. But authentification by the master is necessary.

For beginners, all that matters is the practice of zazen. Don't make categories with your own minds; you are too intelligent for that.

Zen means understanding with the body, and when that happens the master certifies the disciple who has understood more deeply than the others. But if the disciple's everyday life is very bad there is a mistake somewhere and his mind has gone wrong.

Obaku, Muso, and other great Zen masters often said that intellectual understanding of Zen was an obstacle to true understanding. Do you recommend reading or not? Is it dangerous?

It isn't bad, but you must not make mistakes. Sometimes reading is a good thing. If you do nothing but practice zazen your knowledge cannot progress; you must read books, but choose them carefully.

You must not confuse the moon with the finger pointing to it. Tosan burned all his books! Maybe he was too emotional. It was a strong decision. If you read too much you become weak and are always hesitating. But Tosan already knew everything. He had too much learning. So he burned everything and did nothing but practice zazen.

How do we know when we are making a mistake?

I don't know; you must understand for yourself. Think, reflect; that is the best way. You cannot know by any outside means. It's easy to lie to other people but very hard to lie to oneself!

Are koans used in Soto Zen?

Everything is koan. True koans are not play-acting. The master must create questions: What is ku. What is mu? What is your original nature? But when they are used again and again afterward, they become play-acting. The disciples understand only by books. Koan teaching as in Rinzai Zen is not so effective.

In Soto Zen the teacher also uses koans. But "here and now" is most important. These are not university examinations. The only problems are the real problems of everyday life. You suffer, you are worried, you are not satisfied, you are full of questions. And the master answers.

And the answer becomes a koan. I give long explanations and people understand. The answer becomes a question that is a koan. *My answer has become your koan.* It is more effective.

You must not make categories.

Nowadays, in Rinzai Zen, koans have become more like formalities. But the great Rinzai masters did not use koans. Only little masters use them; they read the question before zazen and tell the disciples to think about it during zazen. During zazen the real master says, "You must not think with your brain but with your body." When you study koans you think with your brain.

Everyday life is a koan. "Hello, how are you?" becomes a koan. I can also say, "Chin in" or "Beautiful posture," and that becomes a koan. "Stretch your spine": that's a koan.

During zazen you must not think with your brain. The consciousness of each person is unlimited, infinite. You must let your thoughts pass by and at the end they wear out of their own accord and then you can think unconsciously.

In this day and age people think too much, are too complicated. After zazen their faces have changed and if they continue to practice they become smiling.

After six months or a year of practice everything is completely different. You become light, free, not complicated. Your karma wears out.

What is the use of koans?

They are the words of a master, teaching by means of very simple words which the disciple has to understand by intuition and not by his brain or his learning.

In the Rinzai school koans have become a technique, a formality. You can find the answers in books!

One day a disciple went to the room of my master Kodo Sawaki to talk about a subject that was bothering him.

"Please tell me the essence of Zen, the nature of Buddha," he asked.

"To whom am I supposed to give the answer?" Sawaki replied.

"Tell me, it's a question that is bothering me."

"Tell you!" and he burst out laughing. "Tell you? But you are nothing, you have absolutely no importance."

That is a real koan. A lion's roar in the ear of a chicken.

No more questions?

Then everybody's got satori!

A DIALOGUE WITH CHRISTIAN MONKS

In the course of this mondo, which took place at the Dominican monastery of L'Arbresle, there was a dialogue between the Dominican fathers and Deshimaru Roshi.

I'd like to ask you a question about the disappearance of the ego. There is one aspect of the ego which I can understand easily—that is, the instinctive aspect, the reflex of self-defense: the ego will not yield to correction. But there is another thing which I find harder to understand, and that is the possibility, as you say in Zen, of radically transcending every aspect of the ego.

It is very hard to abandon the ego, and I did not say that it disappeared completely. You can believe in your consciousness or mind that you have abandoned your ego but the body doesn't always agree. By training the body, Zen trains us to let go of the ego. You can suffer during zazen but if you are patient and let go of the pain at the conscious level, and if you repeat that practice regularly, you are unconsciously training yourself to abandon the ego. In thought nothing could be simpler than to abandon the ego, but to let go of it "here and now" is very difficult. Through the repetition of zazen one trains one's body and abandons one's ego unconsciously. That is Zen education.

Can one abandon the ego completely? Isn't that an ideal?

It is very difficult, true. But after all, what is the ego? We have no noumenon, no permanent substance. Our ego has no distinct, permanent existence.

Couldn't one consider abandoning the ego as no different from any other act, working, greeting someone, earning money . . . It would be a greater act, but an act even so?

Abandoning the ego is not so important in everyday actions; but how to abandon the ego in the last moment of life? The concept of sacrifice is not so important in Buddhism. But when we have to die, we have to die.

Can't we give a meaning to our death?

Death is the end. When you have to die you die. "Here and now" is what matters. If somebody is aiming a gun at me my death is "here and now" and without fear. When a person has cancer it's the same thing. One can say to oneself, "I must die." What is important is to make the "decision" to die.

Does the decision have a meaning?

No meaning. It is not necessary to give any special meaning to it; one must die, that's all. It is not in the moment of death that you ask yourself, "How should I die, why should I die?" When you are fighting with two swords in a tournament you don't tell yourself, "I don't want to die! What will happen to me if I lose?" In a fight, body and mind act together and accept death together. To live.

Trying to abandon the ego by thinking about it is extremely hard. But by training the body in zazen we learn to abandon our body, and our anxieties go with it. Through the mind only, it is more difficult because thought is egotistical. By letting go of the body death becomes easy. When we have to die we die, without moving, without anything. But when it is not time for us to die then we had better not do it, we had better run away. That is clear. But I understand what you wanted to say.

The problem is not accepting death but knowing whether one accepts it "here and now."

You can accept death in your thoughts but the body, too, must make that "decision." *You cannot die with the brain only, or by thinking about it.*

Is the body's "decision" the only one that is valid? Why not that of the mind?

It is so difficult for the mind to "decide" death. Even a great master who says, "I want to die now!" in his heart of hearts does not want to die. Christ himself, feeling that his end was near, was not eager to die. That is why we must abandon the body; but even so there always remains a tiny thought of refusal in the brain.

In traditional religions there is always a heaven or paradise or other life after death. That is one way of preparing people for death.

If you think about death in hope of a future life in some Beyond, that is all very well; but if you do not have such beliefs, then you live in fear of the moment when you must get into your coffin. But if "here and now" I must die, if my body accepts death, then my consciousness remains peaceful. If you think about your body before dying, death is difficult. The body does not really "decide" to die. The body is matter, it is not the true me. Nor is my consciousness the true me, because it is constantly changing. We must understand our noumenon, understand that we have no noumenon and that nothing is ultimately important. If we understand that then we needn't bother to try to abandon the ego. What is the ego that understands this? It exists, it is Buddha, God, the highest truth.

How did Buddha die?

Buddha died an old man, over eighty, after eating some wild pig that was not fresh. When he died he was peaceful, without anxiety. When we have to die we die, we go back to the cosmos. When our activity finishes, when our life is over, then we must die. What one must understand is, "Here and now I must die."

Who understands?

The true ego understands. The true ego is the one that makes the decision. The essential problem of all spiritual thinking of real value is to know oneself. The highest philosophy is the philosophy of ku, existence without noumenon. The ego has no noumenon. The consciousness changes incessantly and is without noumenon. Take matter: there is the atom, then neutrons, then even smaller particles, then nothing. In our bodies, too, in the end, there is nothing either, no noumenon. It is the true ego that realizes this.

Little by little, through zazen, immobility, nonthinking, the true ego emerges: it's like looking at oneself in a mirror.

But in reality the true ego is not ego; perhaps it is what in Christianity is known as God. But in Zen it is called true ego, absolute ego. This ego also has no noumenon. It is what understands. Something has to understand and that's the only thing that can, God or the cosmos. It's the self that has let go of everything, the self that has broken its ties with the family, with money, honors, love; the self, too, that has let go of the body, nirvana.

What is the self in Christianity? I often talk about the death of Christ because in Christianity Jesus deliberately gave up his life, by an action. How did God take the "decision" to die in him?

> *Jesus fought a battle among humans. His enemies wanted him to die and he freely accepted death rather than betray his mission. He transformed his death into his mission—that is, the manifestation to humans of love, of the gift of self.*

Perhaps that is how Christ died. But can other men do the same thing? How do you think people should confront death? Christ is different; he decided to die in order to save mankind, but what must other people decide?

> *In the Christian life other people are called to imitate the manner of Jesus's death.*

To help others? How can a person "help" at the moment of death?

> *It is not necessary to give one's life for the love of mankind. There are much simpler things to do to help one's neighbors, things more accessible to people here and now.*

The role of religion is to help people to confront the moment of death. At that final instant, the attitude of body and mind is very important. What should it be? Unconscious acceptance of death. The person who realizes that can live at peace until and in that final moment. That is the teaching of Zen education.

If I understand Zen correctly, it seems to me that it can help more than the body; it can help the whole being to take this decision. But the object of Christianity is to give one's life to God in order to save others.

It is said that after death we go to be with Buddha, that if our life has been perfect we go to Paradise. That can be a way of helping other people. I used to believe that was the way it was. I still do, a little . . . It is very hard to choose.

To die for God or for other people is very different from dying in order to go to Paradise.

There is the *Amida** school of Buddhism in Japan. My mother belonged to it and brought me up in that teaching: there was a paradise beyond death. I don't believe it now but perhaps when the moment comes for me to die I shall think of it again . . .

Some masters, before they died, got up and sat in the zazen posture, some even died standing up. It's a good way to educate your disciples before you die. But perhaps in the moment of my own death my last words to my disciples will be, "I do not want to die." I cannot decide which is the best attitude to have facing death. It is a great koan. After death everything is finished; there is nothing anymore. Until death each person has a consciousness and that consciousness goes on eternally. But in the moment of death what state of mind should we have? During the war I had one experience that was close to death: I had to travel from Japan to Indonesia on a ship loaded with dynamite. On the ship I practiced zazen and when the bombs began to fall I said, "Now I am going to die." If you abandon your body death becomes easier for the consciousness. Then I said to myself, "After death, what am I going to do?" I thought about my family; then it becomes very difficult to "decide" one's own death. If I had been alone it might have been all right, but when I thought about my parents or my family I did not want to die. These tormented thoughts then gave way to calm: "Now and here I am going to die." When one has had the psychological experience of this state one knows the serenity that comes before death.

It is a great problem; we could talk about it for days. It is also the essence of religions. After this experience of death I decided to become a monk. My family is important to me but although it is true that I must help my family, I also have to help other people. But how to help other people to live this moment of death?

Human beings are afraid of dying. They are always running after something: money, honor, pleasure. But if you had to die now, what would you want?

Can religions as they are today give us the answer?

I believe that in the case of Christ what touches me most is not that he died but that he was resurrected.

That is your faith. But some people do not believe that. And how do you help them? It is a great problem.

Supposing a Buddhist no longer had any problems in connection with his own death; what would be his reason for living?

Only the great masters have no fear at all. When they have to die they die. Their lives are devoted to helping others.

Christians also live to help others.

But what does it mean, to help others? Is it making love, giving money? The highest help is giving peace of mind and spirit to people. My master gave me that priceless treasure, the one all people seek.

Seek for others or for themselves?

What is helping? Help how? Help whom? A great koan. If you don't know what "help" means, how can you help? *That is the first problem.*

GLOSSARY

Sanskrit terms are marked (S).

Alaya(S): "reservoir of consciousness." The store-consciousness, the ultimate unconscious, which contains and receives all potentialities and out of which consciousness grows.

Amida school or Amida-butsu: the Jodomon or "Pure Land" teaching developed in Japan by Ryonin (founder of the Nembutsu sect), Honen (founder of the Jodo sect), and Ippen (founder of the Ji sect). Maintains that anyone who invokes the name of Amida Buddha with a sincere heart can achieve rebirth in the pure land.

Anapanasati(S): the harmonious breathing of zazen concentration.

Avalokitesvara(S): (Japanese: Kannon) The bodhisattva of great compassion, who realized his own nature through the ability to listen. He, or she, or what is beyond both, "listens to the sound of the world," and symbolizes the compassion that has vowed to save all sentient beings.

Bodhi tree: the name of the tree under which Buddha attained enlightenment.

Bodhidharma(S): 5th–6th c. A.D., died around 530. The founder of Ch'an (Chinese Zen Buddhism) and first patriarch of the line continuing from Buddha to the present. An Indian monk who settled in China and taught zazen there. Partly legendary but probably existed. According to tradition, when he first came to Shaolin monastery in China he practiced zazen facing a wall for a number of years. Eka was his most important disciple and is said to have cut off his arm to prove his determination to the unmoving patriarch.

Bodhisattva(S): "living Buddha." Anyone can know he or she is that, and devote his or her life to helping other people without leaving "society." There is no visible difference between bodhisattvas and anybody else, but their mind is Buddha.

Bonno: illusion; mental functions which trouble the mind, passions, false views. Desires are natural; they become bonno when there is attachment.

Buddha(S): the Sanskrit root *budh* meant awakening and Buddha is the awakened one. Ordinarily refers to the historical Buddha, Gautama Siddhartha or Shakyamuni, who lived in the 6th c. B.C., but is also applied to all who have attained the highest truth, true freedom. All of us possess the nature of Buddha, the original essence of life.

Dharma(S): according to the Sanskrit root, all processes governing cosmic life, the laws of the universe, known or as yet unknown. Also means the teachings of Buddha, all existences, all truths, cosmic truth, the consequences of action.

Diamond Sutra: *Kongo-kyo.* An early and important sutra which sets forth the doctrines of emptiness and wisdom; one of the basic Zen texts.

Do: the Way, highest truth.

Dogen: 1200–1253 A.D. Founder of the Soto school in Japan. Went to China in 1223 and studied with Master Nyojo, returning to Japan in 1227; built and retired to the temple of Eihei-ji in 1244.

Dojo: place for practice of the way (i.e., zazen).

Fuse: one of the six wisdoms; giving, with no object in mind, and not only material giving.

Fushiryo: not-thinking, as distinct from shiryo (thinking) and hishiryo (beyond thinking) in Dogen's *Fukanzazengi.*

Gassho: salutation, palms joined together with fingertips at mouth level. Not a mark of any particular faith, but a symbol of unity beyond opposites.

Genjokoan: one of the most important passsages of Dogen's *Shobogenzo* (his major work, in ninety-five parts).

Gya tei gya tei: "on, beyond, together beyond"; first part of the mantra which concludes the *Hannya Shingyo* as it has been rendered from Sanskrit into Japanese.

Hannya Shingyo: *Heart Sutra* (S: Mahaprajnaparamita-sutra). The quintessence of a highly elaborated body of sutras (six hundred volumes) and the central text of Mahayana Buddhism. Chanted in all dojos at the end of zazen.

Hara: literally, the intestines; a concentration of nerves as important as that situated at the base of the brain. Zazen and right breathing strengthen the hara, the center of energy and activity.

Hinayana or **Theravada:** not long after the death of Shakyamuni Buddha, his followers divided into two streams, one conservative and the other progressive: the Hinayana (Lesser Vehicle) or Theravada is the more passive stream concentrating on faith and precepts; it is found predominantly in Sri Lanka and Southeast Asia.

Hishiryo: thinking without thoughts, beyond thought. See *fushiryo.*

Hokyo Zanmai: Samadhi of the Treasure-Mirror, by Master Tozan (807–869 A.D.). Important early text, also in everyday use in temples and dojos today.

I shin den shin: "from my soul to your soul"; in other words, transmitted wordlessly.

Jihi: compassion; ji = giving happiness; hi = saving sentient beings from suffering.

Kai: the precepts; their nature and number vary with the ordination (bodhisattva or monk) and, in Japan, with the sex (there are more for women than for men).

Kanji: the old Chinese written character, ideogram. Used by modern Japanese calligraphers.

Kannon: see Avalokitesvara.

Karma(S): literally, action. The chain of causes and effects. The three main kinds of karma are body, mouth (speech), and mind, or consciousness.

Kensho: term used mainly in Rinzai Zen to signify a kind of abrupt awakening or realization, usually after vigorous stimulation.

Kesa: symbol of transmission from master to disciple. The garment worn by the Buddha, now by monks. To make himself a garment after renouncing asceticism, the Buddha went to the banks of the Ganges where the dead were cremated, picked up pieces of winding-sheets, washed them in the river, stained them with ochre-colored clay (*kasaya* means ochre in Sanskrit), and sewed them together. Later, leaves and herbs were used as dyes and mixed so that the pieces of cloth would have muted, blended hues, not pure colors. The seams evoke a rice paddy. The kesa is always sewn by hand and signifies the transformation of the most threadbare and lowliest fabrics into the most beautiful and holy object, just as the most perverse being can become the most awakened one.

Ki: activity, invisible energy of the cosmos, which becomes the energy in all living cells.

Kin-hin: a slow, rhythmic walk between two periods of seated meditation or zazen.

Koan: Initially, a principle of government. As meant by Deshimaru Roshi, a paradoxical question of existence. Also, a principle of eternal truth transmitted by a master.

Kodo Sawaki: 1880–1965. The master of Taisen Deshimaru.

Kolomo: the wide-sleeved black monk's robe.

Ku: emptiness, void, fundamental unsubstantiality. (S: sunyata.)

Kusen: oral teaching during zazen.

Kyosaku: the stick of awakening, used by Zen masters. Administered during zazen between neck and shoulder (trapezius muscles), where many acupuncture meridians intersect and tension often accumulates; its effect is both stimulating and calming.

Lotus Sutra: *Myoho-renge-kyo.* This sutra is virtually worshipped by followers of the Tendai and Nichiren sects.

Mahayana: the Greater Vehicle, or more progressive current, in Buddhism. The active path, in which universal love and work for the salvation of mankind figure prominently. Flourished mainly in China, Tibet, and Japan.

Manas(S): a level of consciousness, the root of all illusion.

Manjusri(S): Monju-Bosatsu in Japanese. The bodhisattva of meditation or supreme wisdom.

Mondo: questions and answers between master and disciples.

Mu: absolute nothing; gramatically, a negative prefix, un- or non-.

Mujo: impermanence; the condition of everything in the universe.

Mushin: no-mind. See shin.

Mushotoku: without any goal or profit-seeking.

Nagarjuna: regarded as the patriarch of most schools of Japanese Buddhism. Lived in India 2nd c. A.D. The first to formulate the doctrine of ku and the middle way. Author of commentary on the *Hannya Shingyo.*

Nirvana(S): total extinction of phenomena. Sometimes synonymous with death.

Rakusu: a small kesa worn by monks for work and by bodhisattvas.

Rinzai: after Eno in China (700 A.D.), five schools formed, using different methods of education. Two have survived, Rinzai and Soto. The former makes more intensive use of koans; zazen, which is practiced facing the center of the dojo, has become essentially a means of obtaining satori.

Samadhi(S): concentration (Zanmai in Japanese).

Sampai: prostration, the forehead touching the ground and the palms facing upward on either side of the head (symbolically to receive the Buddha's feet); the sign of profound respect, reverence.

Samu: physical work, performed with great concentration.

Sangha(S): the master and disciples, the community of people practicing.

Satori(S): awakening. Sometimes translated illumination, enlightenment, realization; "normal condition."

Sesshin: a period of intensive zazen training; can last one or two days or several weeks or months. Group living in concentration and silence, with four–five (or more) hours of zazen a day interspersed with lectures, mondos, manual work, and meals.

Shakyamuni: see Buddha.

Shikantaza: "only sit." Concentration on the practice of zazen.

Shiki: phenomena, forms, visible entities.

Shiki soku ze ku, ku soku ze shiki: core sentence of the *Hannya Shingyo,* translated by Deshimaru Roshi. "Phenomena become (are not different from) ku, ku becomes (is not different from) phenomena."

Shin: heart, soul, spirit, mind, intuition. And more.

Shin Jin Mei: *Poem on Faith in Zazen,* by Master Sosan (d. 606).

Shodoka: *The Song of Immediate Satori,* by Yoka Daishi (d. 713 A.D.).

Shobogenzo: *Treasure of the True Law* (among other translations); the main work by Master Dogen.

Soto: in the Soto school, that of Deshimaru Roshi, zazen is practiced without any goal or object, facing the wall. The master does not systematically assign koans to students; his replies to their questions become koans.

Sutra(S): the teachings of the Buddha, transmitted by his disciples. Immensely expounded and elaborated over the centuries to incorporate all the circumstances with which Buddhism has had to contend as it moved from place to place and period to period. A vast literature embodying the teachings of all the masters.

Teisho: oral transmission of the Dharma in lecture form.

Theravada(S): see Hinayana.

Uji: chapter of Dogen's *Shobogenzo,* on the nature of time.

Zafu: a firm cushion filled with kapok, on which one sits to practice zazen. Without a zafu, the knees are not firmly pressed against the ground and the back cannot be sufficiently straight.

Zen: Dhyana in Sanskrit, Ch'an in Chinese; true, profound silence. Usually translated as concentration or objectless meditation. Return to the pure, original mind.